GOOD ENGLISH

TEACH YOURSELF

GOOD ENGLISH

A PRACTICAL BOOK OF SELF-INSTRUCTION IN
ENGLISH COMPOSITION BASED ON THE WORK BY
G. H. THORNTON, M.A., COMPLETELY REVISED AND
ENLARGED BY KATHLEEN BARON, B.A.

THE ENGLISH UNIVERSITIES PRESS LTD
ST. PAUL'S HOUSE WARWICK LANE
LONDON · E.C.4

First printed in this form 1938
This impression 1968

This is published in the U.S.A. by David McKay
Company Inc., 750 Third Avenue, New York,
N.Y. 10017

S.B.N. 340 05792 0

Printed and Bound in Great Britain for the English Universities Press, Ltd.,
by Richard Clay (The Chaucer Press), Ltd., Bungay, Suffolk

INTRODUCTION

This book attempts to examine the principles that underlie good written English, and to suggest the best methods by which you may learn to write good English yourself.

This is a vaguer task than the grammarian's, and one more difficult to accomplish. He deals with language after it has been written down, and makes his rules to fit with current practice, not to guide it. Like the student of anatomy, his work is to probe and dissect, and he has a whole dictionary of terms by which he may label whatever he finds. To know these labels will not help you to write good English. You may be learned in all the uses of restrictive and illative and copulative clauses, and yet be unable to compose a single sentence with lucidity and ease. The study of formal grammar is useful in itself, but it will no more help you to write than a knowledge of anatomy will help a lame man to walk. This book therefore tries to avoid grammatical labels as far as possible, though in discussing sentence-structure it has sometimes been necessary to borrow them. It aims at showing the processes of prose construction, and once you understand them and have practised them for yourselves, you have no need to know the grammarian's names for them. To have talked much and read much is of more value in learning to write good English than to have parsed and analysed half a library.

Yet, you may ask, how far can good writing

be taught? It is clearly a different problem from teaching arithmetic or Latin or trigonometry. In all these subjects you may lay down definite rules, but English, written as well as spoken, is both personal and instinctive. In learning to write, you are learning to express *yourself*; if you write well, whatever you write will be plainly and unmistakably your own. It seems therefore almost as difficult to write a book on composition as it must be to write those popular and fascinating handbooks on how to cultivate your personality. The problem is fundamentally the same. Professor Raleigh is extremely severe towards all such writers: "When you go to the teachers of composition, they cannot tell you what to say. They wait until you have said something and then they carp at it. They help you to a good style about as much as detectives help a thief to a good life."

Yet, with deference to Professor Raleigh, there are many ways in which such a book as this may be useful. You learn to compose by stages, learning first to express yourself in simple sentences and to give them variety, then to link your simple sentences into longer ones, and finally to link these into a paragraph. In this way you are able to practise and perfect your writing at each stage, and so to avoid the lop-sided, ungainly style of the man who writes upon instinct as the words come into his head. In considering vocabulary, and in examining examples of bad writing, you sharpen your critical sense, and in the practice of précis and paraphrase you gain accuracy and conciseness, while in the later chapters you will find advice on tackling essays, descriptions and stories. By the time you have worked through this book, you will have absorbed the principles of good writing, and you will insensibly put them into practice. Most valuable of all, your study will have taught you how to criticise your own work, and you will have no need of a teacher, since you will rarely find a severer critic than yourself.

Some of the exercises set require criticism or correction of style; others demand original writing. The first can generally be checked by the Key; for the second, it is only possible to provide specimen compositions which will serve as a standard, and illustrate a different method of approaching the same subject. You cannot be too strongly urged not to look at the Key until you have finished your own exercise, however strong the temptation. Nothing more effectively paralyses the mind than to read what someone else has written on the same subject. Never be content to answer a question in your head; to write down an answer requires clearer thinking and more precise expression, and clearness and precision are qualities indispensable to any writer.

If it is at all possible, work with another student. You will find that each stimulates the other, and in criticising another's work you become more critical of your own. But, most important of all, you must yourself continually practise writing, not only formal composition, but letters, diaries—anything that offers freedom of self-expression. Without this constant practice you will never be able to write well or fluently, but, having learnt all the graces and arts of style, will be left disconsolate with nothing at all to say.

CONTENTS

CONTENTS

CONTENTS

xiv

PART I

MEANING OF COMPOSITION—METHOD OF STUDY

Composition is simply the art of saying what we mean—an art which sounds easier than it really is, as we may remember from the Hatter's remarks in *Alice in Wonderland* :—

" ' Do you mean that you think you can find out the answer to it ? ' said the March Hare.

" ' Exactly so,' said Alice.

" ' Then you should say what you mean,' the March Hare went on.

" ' I do,' Alice hastily replied, ' at least—at least I mean what I say—that's the same thing, you know.'

" ' Not the same thing a bit ! ' said the Hatter. ' Why, you might just as well say that " I see what I eat " is the same thing as " I eat what I see " ! ' "

That is excellent logic, and if it is a little difficult to follow, it serves to illustrate the essential difficulty of all composition—of saying what we really mean.

For most of us, the study of composition begins at the age of two or thereabouts. A child begins to talk by saying single words, then, guided by instinct and imitation, learns to compose words into sentences, sentences into continuous speech. This process of composition is natural and unconscious, and he learns with astonishing ease.

Written composition carries the process a stage further, and it is less easy because less instinctive, though it is in its essentials the same. Here again he is guided by instinct, but still more by imitation, and this time he unconsciously imitates not speech, but what he has read. A Somerset child will speak with a Somerset accent because he hears it on every side. So, in the same way, in learning to write he will naturally adopt the style and vocabulary of the books and papers he reads most often.

In the past, the Authorised Version of the Bible profoundly influenced speech and writing, because it was the staple literature of the common people. The ignorant tinker who wrote *The Pilgrim's Progress* wrote great prose because his ear was attuned to the language and cadence of the English Bible. To-day, the daily newspaper has taken its place. Instead of David's lament over Jonathan, we read " Scenes in Stepney " or " Love Tragedy in Hyde Park ". It would, of course, be foolish to condemn all newspaper-English as bad. There is much good, vigorous prose written daily in the papers. In clearness and brevity you can learn much from the journalist; in the vivid presentment of facts his is a master hand. The conditions of his work do not permit him to consider the nicety or accuracy of the words he uses, nor is a finely balanced style or intricate sentence-structure well suited to an article which will be read over a hurried breakfast or in a crowded bus or train.

If you wish to gain a good and flexible style, newspapers must not be your only reading, nor must you read them too much. Such a style can only be learnt from good and careful writers.

Read as much and as carefully as you can, and your style will insensibly be influenced by what you read. For critical reading, essays are perhaps the best study, and a book of selected essays [1] offers you great variety of style. The essays of Addison, Hazlitt, Leigh Hunt, Macaulay, R. L. Stevenson, Richard Jeffries, and W. H. Hudson are good models; so also are the essays of contemporary writers such as Robert Lynd, E. V. Lucas, H. M. Tomlinson, Aldous Huxley, Sir Arthur Quiller-Couch. [2] These names are selected from many others because they offer examples of good, direct prose, for it is best at this stage not to study authors who have a markedly individual style. Their mannerisms are easily imitated, while their essential qualities are forgotten. For this reason, essayists such as Lamb, De Quincey, Carlyle, Pater, Max Beerbohm, G. K. Chesterton, Virginia Woolf, are best reserved for later pleasure, when your own style is so far developed that it will not easily be influenced. For general reading, choose novels that are acknowledged to be well-written. You cannot read too much of that fastidious stylist, Robert Louis Stevenson; Thackeray will be good reading at this stage, while Dickens is too " mannered " a writer; but, if you prefer modern novels, you have abundant choice. The best are easily obtainable in cheap editions, and with so wide a choice, selection would be invidious. Study the book reviews in the newspaper, or consult your local librarian, if you do not know which to choose. You cannot always read slowly and critically, and your enjoyment

[1] Such as *English Essays* (World's Classics Series).
[2] Cf. *English Essay of To-day* (Oxford University Press).

of a novel would be spoiled by such a treatment. Yet nevertheless you should try every day to read a page or so of good prose slowly and with attention, noting the value of the words chosen and the rhythm and construction of the sentences. Good prose does not merely convey a clear meaning, but is written to satisfy the ear. To gain its full effect, you must read a passage aloud, so that its rhythm stays in your head like a remembered tune and your own style unconsciously takes on some of its music and balance.

The study of good prose is important in developing your critical sense and moulding your style, but study is not enough. You must constantly practise writing for yourself, and, if you wish to write well, you will not be content merely to work through the exercises in this book. This constant practice is less difficult than it sounds. Every letter you write offers you an opportunity, and the fact that someone else must read what you have written enforces a sufficiently exacting standard. Letters are especially useful in teaching you a sense of appropriateness, which is essential for success in writing. You instinctively adapt your style to your correspondent, just as in writing essays you will have to adapt your style to your subject. If you have little opportunity for letter-writing, then the next best course is to keep a diary—not the kind of diary that one used to receive at Christmas, with one half-inch of space in which to record all the pleasures, excitements and miseries of the day, but one in which you may write at ease, and may set down whatever interesting things you have done or seen or heard. The value of keeping a diary is that you may write in it without self-consciousness, with no thought that anyone else may read it. Pepys, writing carelessly for his own diversion, produced one of the pleasantest works in the world. Here is an extract from his diary for 1660 :—

"After dinner we went to the Green Dragon on Lambeth Hill, and there we sang of all sorts of things, and I ventured with good success upon things at first sight, and after that I played on my flageolet, and staid there till nine o'clock, very merry and drawn on with one song after another till it came to be so late. So parted and thence home, where I found my wife and maid a-washing. I staid up till the bellman came by with his bell just under my window as I was writing of this very line, and cried, 'Past one of the clock, and a cold, frosty, windy morning'. I then went to bed, and left my wife and the maid a-washing still."

Yet you may feel perhaps that you do not live so active or so "merry" a life as Mr. Pepys —that you have, in short, nothing to write about. There lies the root problem of all composition, and you cannot find the solution from books. A man who had lived all his life in his study, with only books for friends, would never be a great writer, even though he acquired by practice all the arts of style. Writing is the translation into words of thought and sensation and experience. If you use well your faculties of eye and ear, if you multiply and deepen your interests, then you will find the stimulus and the material for writing, and the eagerness of your thought will forge your style.

Your study should be divided between reading,

writing, and the formal lessons given in this book. It will be best at first to spend most time upon the work in this book, so that when you are writing for yourself you may put into practice the elementary rules given in the first thirteen lessons. The initial requirement in all writing is that you should say what you mean with clearness and accuracy. These are the first virtues to be cultivated; without them all elegance of style is worthless. They can be gained only by systematic practice, and for this reason the lessons of this book are arranged in systematic order, so that you will use simple sentences before you go on to more complicated constructions. When you have worked through a lesson, consider your own writing in the light of what you have learnt, and amend it where you can. Periodic revision of your work is a useful practice, but you should always allow some time to elapse before you attempt this critical survey of what you have written. When you have just finished a piece of work, especially if it has cost you a good deal of trouble, you are in no position to judge of its merits. One or two comparatively insignificant words—a *nor* or an *if*, a *this* or a *then*—have been so carefully considered that they practically dwarf their more important fellows. The whole passage is out of focus. Later—perhaps after a week or more—you will be able to judge the passage as a whole.

Although in the correction of faulty sentences given in the exercises, and in the detailed criticism of your own work, you must bear in mind the rules of grammar and style, you must try not to let them assume too much importance. By degrees, correct expression will come naturally without any conscious attention to rules. They must never at any time be too rigidly applied, for pedantry and good writing never go together. Even Shakespeare has sorely troubled the grammarians. The strict laws of grammar need not always be insisted on, if the meaning is clear and the expression conforms with current practice. Do not be like the Victorian lady who was so conscious of correct grammar that, when she received a letter from her husband beginning, " My dearest Maria ", she replied, " My dear John, I beg that you will either mend your morals or your grammar. You call me your *dearest* Maria; am I to understand that you have other Marias? "

LESSON I

VOCABULARY—WORDS AND THEIR VALUE

Words are the raw material of the writer's craft, and in his choice of them lies very much of his skill. English offers him an immense vocabulary, enriched from many sources. French and Latin have added most to the original Saxon stock, but words have been borrowed from almost every country under the sun. French came over with the Norman conquerors; Renaissance scholars borrowed direct from Latin and Greek; fine gentlemen in Elizabeth's day garnished their speech with French, Italian and Spanish phrases; merchants and sailors and adventurers brought home new words from East and West. The process has been continuous, and continues still to-day. By these means the

English vocabulary has increased not only in size, but in richness and variety. There seems at times a bewildering number of words which might express one plain meaning. How, then, shall we select the right one?

To the writer, words have value in three different ways. Most important, of course, is the meaning. He will choose the word that seems to express most accurately what he has to say. Yet he may find that several words seem to serve his turn equally well, so that he has to consider them in two other ways—for their sound and their association.

Though the practice of reading aloud is almost dying out, you must not think of the written word as a mere collection of letters on the printed page. When we read to ourselves, we hear in imagination the sound of what we are reading. Silent reading cannot destroy the sound-value of words, and the careful writer will consider not only their individual sound, but how far that sound fits into the rhythm or musical pattern of the sentence. In the passage Pater has written on the portrait of Mona Lisa not a word could be changed without destroying the music of the whole :--

" She is older than the rocks among which she sits ; like the vampire, she has been dead many times, and learned the secrets of the grave ; and has been a diver in deep seas, and keeps their fallen day about her. . . ."

Some words express sounds in themselves, and have been coined in imitation of the sounds they express. *Rustle, whisper, hush, chatter, whimper,* are examples, and you can find many more, if you think (and listen) carefully. They have a special value in suggesting a sound almost directly to the imagination, and for this reason they are much used in poetry and in vivid descriptive prose.

Words are no less important for their associations than for their sounds. A word takes on colour and character according to the way it is used. From being commonly used to express a certain idea, it is always associated in the mind with that idea. You might write *The priest chuckled*, but you would feel a certain impropriety in writing *The priest giggled*, since we associate that word with the schoolgirl, and do not use it in any flattering sense. Words are constantly gathering new associations : some gain dignity, others lose it ; some are mysterious, some matter-of-fact. You must read widely and attentively if you would be aware of the subtle changes that words undergo in their journeyings.

If in writing you are to find the best words and use them well, then you must have as many words as possible at your disposal. The vocabulary of everyday speech is meagre. Comparatively few words are needed to explain material wants ; primitive people make do with very few. Civilisation increases man's vocabulary by increasing his knowledge and his needs ; but it is when man begins to think that he needs more words to express his ideas and opinions. Still more are needed when he comes to write them down. The vocabulary of speech and that of writing differ widely in scope, and words that seem forceful in speech seem vague and unconvincing when written. You may say emphatically, " This play is rotten ", but if you are asked to write down your opinion, you will have to search for more precise words in which to express it. You may write instead, " This play is badly constructed, badly written and badly acted ". These are common enough words, but you have had to pause a moment before finding them. Every time that you make this effort towards clearer thought and exacter expression, you will find that the right words come more easily.

If you are to have the best vocabulary for your purpose, you must constantly enlarge it by careful reading. Do not pass over any word whose meaning is not quite clear, for until you know a word in all its meanings, it is dangerous to use it. Aldous Huxley has a pleasant story of a young man who fell in love with the word " carminative ", which he found on the label of a cinnamon bottle. He treasured it for its warmth and colour and sound, and used it at last in a poem to his lady, in which he expressed the carminative quality of his passion. It was a mere accident that he looked it up in the dictionary and discovered, to his grief and vexation, that it meant " good for curing flatulence ".[1]

In reading use a dictionary to discover the meaning of a word; use your own critical instinct to estimate its worth. Read a piece of good prose over slowly and savour the words as you go; or, even better, read poetry, for the poet even more than the writer of prose must be aware of the sound and atmosphere of the words he uses. Poets who use a definitely poetic vocabulary will be of small use for this purpose,

[1] *Chrome Yellow*, Aldous Huxley.

but read those poets whose vocabulary is fairly close to that of modern prose.[1]

Once you are familiar with their correct use in prose use the words you have learnt, but do not in your enthusiasm use your choicest words too often. Like jewels, they are made more beautiful by their rarity. They are more effective when used with restraint. One or two rich words will lend fineness and distinction to a paragraph, where more will only weary those who read it. Shakespeare, in *Macbeth*, deliberately sets two echoing words among a crowd of plain, short ones :—

" What hands are here? ha ! they pluck out my
    eyes !
Will all great Neptune's ocean wash this blood
Clean from my hand? No ; this my hand will
    rather
The *multitudinous seas incarnadine*
Making the green, one red."

Finally, never go to the dictionary for new words, for you cannot learn from it how to use them, and will inevitably use them wrongly.

Exercise I

(a) In the following sentences, replace the words printed in italics by more suitable words, and indicate your reasons for the change :—

1. One statesman thought the treaty *derogative* to his country's honour. 2. The Frenchman regards the *observation* of the Sabbath from a different standpoint than we do. 3. The town officials did their best to make the tram-

[1] As, for instance, Coleridge, Keats, Wordsworth, Browning, and almost any of the contemporary poets.

cars popular and *payable*. 4. Among the domestics she raised such *dissent* that no pair of them remained on speaking terms. 5. Your best plan is to treat her as *contemptibly* as you can. 6. Like all Scotsmen he maintained that porridge is the most *healthy* food. 7. It seemed, therefore, that Dirk ought to *decease*. 8. One of that great army of cooks sent by the devil for the *spoliation* of God's food. 9. The girl was *sick with nostalgia*. 10. By these remarks do you mean to *infer* that I know something about your miserable savings? 11. I have photographed the children of that school now for thirty years without a *breakage*. 12. The island of Ceylon is famous for its *luxurious* vegetation. 13. The *acceptation* of the sword of honour from the council does not commit the general to their policy. 14. The murderer was seen in the very *action* of firing his gun. 15. After the *invention* of chloroform, surgical operations had a much greater chance of success. 16. The body was so mangled that it could hardly be recognised as *humane*.

(b) Write down ten adjectives which you might use to describe a country stream.

Write down ten adjectives which you might use to describe a river flowing through a city.

(Think of the appearance, movement and sound of the water in each case.)

LESSON II

VOCABULARY—SYNONYMS

The advantage of a wide vocabulary is that you may express your thoughts with precision and grace. It is also occasionally useful in enabling you to avoid awkward repetition of the same word or sound, by substituting one word for another. It is bad to repeat the same word in two different senses, as in these examples :—

The sailors hoisted sail and sailed away.

If you do not stop crying at once you will cause your husband much needless anxiety : I promise you I have his cause at heart.

It is nevertheless even worse to make obvious efforts to avoid repetition. No sensible person would write : *The beautiful girl descended the staircase; he felt he had never seen such a lovely maiden.* But a great many people are strangely shy of repeating the same noun or proper name, and will write *our hero, the anxious husband, the handsome commander,* in the course of a single page, when all the time they merely mean *John Smith.* Your best rule is never to avoid repetition when avoidance of it is obvious.

When one word can be replaced by another, these words are said to be *synonyms,* a clumsy name for words that are similar in meaning. No word can be the exact equivalent of another, as we tried to show in the last lesson, for every word is slightly changed by its use and association. *Behaviour* and *deportment,* for instance, might seem from the dictionary to be almost interchangeable; but, if you consider them, you will find that *deportment* has a narrower meaning, and has grown rather prim through its association with Victorian standards of correctness and good manners. *Snapdragon* and *antirrhinum* are exact equivalents in meaning, but *snapdragon* is the more vivid word for general use, while *antirrhinum* is in place in a technical article on botany or gardening. *Linden* and *lime* are another pair with identical meanings, but in ordinary prose the commoner word *lime* will generally be preferable to the rarer, more poetic word *linden*.

Many so-called synonyms differ also in grammatical use. *Answer*, *reply*, *respond* are commonly called synonyms, yet they cannot be used in exactly the same way. We can say : *He answered her never a word* but not *He responded her never a word*.

English is rich in synonyms, and for this there is an historical reason. The English language is fundamentally Saxon : that is, its grammar is Saxon, and so are all the really essential words. It borrowed words from the Norman conquerors, who brought with them a higher standard of civilisation,[1] but a still larger part of our vocabulary comes from Latin, from which we still continue to borrow. Generally the Latin words are longer and more learned in sound and association than those that come to us from Saxon or direct from French. All the essential words in English are Saxon in origin—*the*, *with*, *of*, *out*, and all the other small necessary words on which language depends. Saxon gives us many words for concrete things—like *milk*, *fish*, *cattle*, *house*; many good words, too, to express simple emotions—*love*, *friendship*, *hate*—but very few indeed to express abstract things or subtle conceptions. These we have had to borrow from French and Latin.

[1] It is interesting to notice that our words for animals are plain Saxon—cow, calf, sheep, oxen—but our words for meat are French in origin—beef (*bœuf*), mutton (*mouton*), veal (*veau*), etc., the reason being that the Normans were not only more cultured, but also better cooks.

In writing prose, we inevitably use many words of Saxon origin, and they will always outnumber the rest, even in books written in what is called a Latin diction—in Dr. Johnson's essays, or Gibbon's history, or books written on scientific subjects. How far you will use words taken from Latin will depend very much on what you are writing. You will use less in a story of action than in an essay on Truth or Justice. In the following passage, taken from the eighteenth-century novel *Tristram Shandy*, Sterne uses few Latin words. A baby has just been born, and Susannah, the maid, is sent to inquire by what name it shall be christened :—

" ' Were one sure,' said my father to himself, scratching his eyebrow, ' that the child was expiring . . . it would be a pity in such a case to throw away so great a name as *Trismegistus* upon him—but he may recover.'

" ' No, no,' said my father to Susannah, ' I'll get up.'

" ' There is no time,' cried Susannah, ' the child's as black as my shoe.'

" ' *Trismegistus*,' said my father. ' But stay ! Thou art a leaky vessel, Susannah,' added my father. ' Canst thou carry *Trismegistus* in thy head the whole length of the gallery without scattering ? '

" ' Can I ? ' cried Susannah, shutting the door in a huff.

" ' If she can, I'll be shot,' said my father, bouncing out of bed in the dark, and groping for his breeches.

" Susannah ran with all speed along the gallery.

" My father made all speed to find his breeches.

" Susannah got the start and kept it. ' 'Tis

Tris—something,' cried Susannah. 'There is no Christian name in the world,' said the curate, 'beginning with *Tris*—but *Tristram*.'

" ' Then 'tis *Tristram-gistus*,' quoth Susannah.

" ' There is no *gistus* to it, noodle !—'tis my own name,' replied the curate, dipping his hand, as he spoke, into the basin. 'Tristram ! ' said he, etc., etc., etc., etc., so Tristram was I called, and Tristram shall I be to the day of my death. . . .''

Compare this with a characteristic passage from one of Johnson's essays, where the sentences are weighted with Latin :—

" It is asserted by Horace, that ' if matter be once got together, words will be found with very little difficulty '; a position which, though sufficiently plausible to be asserted in poetical precepts, is by no means strictly and philosophically true. If words were naturally and necessarily consequential to sentiments, it would always follow, that he who has most knowledge must have most eloquence, and that every man would clearly express what he fully understood.''

Though you may prefer Sterne to Dr. Johnson, it is clearly impossible to say that one kind of diction is better than another. The only test is its appropriateness. Students are sometimes advised to use words of Latin derivation as little as possible. It is felt that they may be so delighted with long Latin words that they will use them in and out of season, and so develop as pompous and pedantic style. Yet it is often as stilted and pedantic to use a Saxon for a Latin word as a Latin word for a Saxon. No sensible person will speak of *lactation* when he means *milking*, but the earnest people who tried to establish the Saxon coinage *folk-wain*, in place of the Latin *omnibus*, were surely equally absurd.

Do not use long Latin words where simpler words will do, but do not strain after an artificial simplicity. If you find in writing that you are using a great many Latin words, it is time to stop and consider what you have written. It is much easier to write nonsense when you are using long Latin words than when you write in plain Saxon. Their weightiness is deceptive, and may conceal the flimsiest of meanings. Examples of such a style can often be found in the leading articles of the daily papers, and it has been amusingly parodied in C. E. Montague's novel, *A Hind Let Loose*. Read it, and you will be ever after on your guard against using pompous words to conceal a pitiful lack of meaning.

Exercise 2

(*a*) In the following sentences supply a synonym for each of the words printed in italics, indicating in each case the slight change of meaning implied by the use of the new word. 1. I shall be glad if you send me the third volume of Campbell's Architecture, and with it any other *entertaining* books. 2. " Well, young gentleman," says a man that stood at the door, " you look *wishfully*." 3. The Greeks took the city of Troy by *guile*. 4. Bute and the *adjacent* island of Arran form one county. 5. Warren Hastings was a *resolute* man. 6. Some of the worst *offenders* were caught and punished. 7. A tear to grace his *obsequies*. 8. I am greatly *indebted* to you for your kindness. 9. A man never *outlives* his conscience. 10. Some students were killed in an affray that took place at a *wedding*. 11. *Globes* of light appeared among the trees. 12. Those tyrants who have been a *reproach* to human nature. 13. Religion *intrenches* upon none of our privileges. 14. The lie that flatters I *abhor* the most. 15. Then *shrieked* the timid and stood still the brave. 16. Carlyle's manuscripts were scarcely *legible*.

(*b*) Write down ten adjectives you might use to describe a policeman, ten more to describe a speaker at an open-air meeting. (Think of their appearance, character, qualities, moods.)

LESSON III

VOCABULARY—CHOICE OF WORDS

When we speak, we suit our words to those to whom we speak; in writing, we address a wide, yet undefined audience, and must use words which will be generally understood. It follows that certain words must be excluded from our written vocabulary since their meaning will not be clear to everyone. They fall into four classes :—

(1) Slang words form the largest class, and though they are often vivid and effective in speech, there are good reasons why they should not be used in writing. Consider first what we mean by slang. *The Concise Oxford Dictionary* defines it thus :—

"Words and phrases in common colloquial use, but generally considered in some or all of their senses to be outside of standard English;

words and phrases either entirely peculiar to, or used in special senses by, some class or profession."

The important part of the definition lies for us in the words " outside standard English ", by which we mean the English that is spoken and understood by the greatest number of educated people. Burglars, in their profession, use a very vivid and effective slang, yet, since their profession is a narrow one, it is, for the writer's purpose, useless. Slang words, if they really supply a gap in language, will one day be accepted in standard English. Till then they should be avoided in ordinary prose.

(2) Words and phrases used only in certain districts are to be avoided for the same reason. They are excellent in speech, and have often much more character than the corresponding words in standard English, yet, since they will not be generally understood, it is unwise to use them. The Scotsman may talk of his " pinkie ", but he will write " little finger "; he may use " wee " in speech, but he will use " little " or " small " in writing. Some local words, like the Scotch " caddie ", have passed into general use, but till then they must be excluded from written English.

(3) Foreign words and phrases should be used as little as possible, unless they have already been absorbed into the language. *Route*, *chauffeur*, *chef*, *matinée* are French words that we could hardly do without. Many other foreign words come into favour from time to time and then pass out of use. *Fuhrer*, *coup*, *putsch*, *duce* are modern examples which the journalist has brought to popular notice. They

TEACH YOURSELF GOOD ENGLISH

are not really necessary in English, and it is
unwise to use them, for their popularity may
quickly fade and their meaning be forgotten.
To use foreign words which will not be known by
people who have not learnt a foreign language is
affected and ill-mannered. Unless you are
writing for a small class of people whom you
know will understand you, this should at all
costs be avoided.

(4) Technical words easily creep into prose if
the writer is a specialist in any subject. It
would be impossible, of course, to write a
technical work without them, but they should
be avoided in general writing.

Words of these four classes are to be avoided,
lest they obscure your meaning; but there is a
fifth class which must be as rigorously avoided
if you wish to write good prose. To this class
belong all words and phrases that have been so
staled by use that they have lost their vividness
and accuracy. For these the journalist is much
to blame, for, writing in haste, he is tempted to
use words as ciphers to fill up a line, very often
using an epithet as makeweight. For him every
crime becomes a *dastardly crime*, every love
affair *tragic* or *romantic*; *grave developments are
awaited* in *the political arena*; *crises* are *averted*
at *the psychological moment*; calm *ensues*;
unhappy wives make *revelations*. Hack words
and phrases are created by bad writing.
Examples might be endless—the misused word
transpire;[1] *partake* (and its falsely refined
passive form—*tea was partaken of*); *in the sphere*

---

[1] *Transpire* means " emerge from secrecy into knowledge,
become known by degrees ". It is frequently wrongly used
with the meaning " happen, turn out ".

of ; *under the circumstances* ; *seriously inclined to* ; *young hopefuls*. You may find countless others for yourself. Such words and phrases are to be avoided if you would write fresh, vigorous prose. If you find yourself using one, look it up in the dictionary, and if you are not using it in its exact sense, strike it out.

Words have a strong tendency to coalesce, to form compounds, and thus to lose their identity. This is essential if each sentence is not to be built up by the conscious effort of joining separate words. These connections should only be the commonplace ones, which are natural and fitting. If you do not know what a man means, you say, without conscious thought, " What do you mean ? " which is natural and fitting. But very often words fall into set phrases, which were once witty or imaginative, but have lost their lustre through overmuch quotation. Shakespeare has contributed many : *Patience on a monument* ; *my prophetic soul !* ; *the pity of it* ; *there's the rub* ; *a snapper-up of unconsidered trifles*; *to be or not to be*; *here's metal more attractive*. These are but a few. Other phrases once witty have become merely facetious—*better half* ; *conspicuous by their absence* ; *the curate's egg* ; *the inner man*, etc. Others have become current journalese—*the logic of events* ; *the irony of fate* ; *the defects of his qualities* ; *leave severely alone*, etc. Such set phrases are to be avoided; if you can invent neat phrases instead of them, well and good; if not, then stick to the plain noun and let the wearied epithet go in peace.

Exercise 3

Express the following sentences in what you feel is a better form :—

1. The Opposition must buck up if they wish to gain anything at the approaching election. 2. The judges were escorted to their hotel with all the pomp and circumstance of war. 3. In the dim, religious light of the pit he could not see to read his programme. 4. Mr. Parkins of this city last night passed over to the other side. 5. It is rumoured that the green-eyed monster was at the bottom of the tragedy that transpired at Gudburgh last night. 6. A cold collation was partaken of by the distinguished party at the witching hour. 7. The authorities were shocked when they learned how the newcomers had painted the town red. 8. The Government is rotten from gunwale to garboard streak. 9. *Al fresco* meals were for him ever the best. 10. The Countess is expecting a happy event shortly. 11. Do not burn the midnight oil over this exercise. 12. I drink cocoa every night as regularly as clockwork. 13. In the sphere of science Einstein is pre-eminent. 14. He suffers from an acute inferiority complex. 15. She declared she loved the little feathered songsters. 16. Greater development of uncorrupted conduct is a desideratum. 17. A really mondaine child now requires an engagement book in which to record her numerous social activities. 18. I am staggered by the impertinence of the honourable member who has just spoken. 19. Now is the psychological moment for the restoration of the monarchy. 20. His book will repay perusal.

LESSON IV

THE SENTENCE—MEANING

Words are the material with which composition deals, but words are not the units of composition. Some words, it is true, can express complete thoughts. Thus *Yes, Never, Listen,* may express a complete thought each. But this is exceptional. In most cases we require several words to communicate a complete thought. Even such words as *Yes* and *Never* depend upon previous words to help out their apparently independent meaning.

A group of words so arranged as to express a complete thought is called a sentence. Sometimes we have a sentence defined as a combination of words making complete sense. By "complete" we must not understand that a sentence tells us all that is to be said, but only that the sense is complete so far as that independent group of words is concerned. Examples of "incomplete sense" will be found below. The following are sentences : *All the world's a stage. I remember. Where do you buy your books ?* If you examine these, or any other sentences, you will find that they always consist of two parts : something spoken about, and something said about it. The words indicating what is spoken about form what is called the *subject* : the words indicating what is said about the subject form what is called the *predicate.* Thus *All the world* is the subject ; *is a stage* is the predicate. *I* is subject ; *remember,* predicate.

In the third sentence we seem to have two subjects ; for we are saying something about *you*

37

B

and also something about *books*. Grammarians, however, are quite clear that *you* is the subject, while *do buy your books where* is the predicate. To understand why *you* is at once selected as the subject, we must consider how it is related to the verb. At first sight it appears as if the verb *buy* were as closely related to *books* as to *you*, but, as a matter of fact, *buy* is more dependent upon *you* than upon *books*. Let us take the sentence in its plain form as a statement, not as a question : *You buy your books*. Here you may change *books* into *book*, or into *clothes*, or *pencils*, or *potatoes*, without in any way changing the rest of the sentence. But if we change *you* into *he* we must change the verb. It must now read *he buys*. In other words, the verb is limited by the subject in regard to *number* and *person*.

> I have a book.
> Thou hast a book.
> She has a book.

Here *I*, *thou* and *she* are the subjects, since they cause the verb to change, while *book* is called the object. We can change the object as much as we please without changing the verb at all. *He sees*—which is the third person singular of the verb—may be followed by *me*, which is first person singular, or *thee*, which is second person singular, or *us*, which is first person plural, or *them*, which is third person plural, or by any sort of objective noun or pronoun.

All parts of the verb which can be thus affected by the number and person of the subject are called *finite* parts. The parts that are not finite are the infinitive and the participles. These do not change with their subjects, because, as a matter of fact, they do not have subjects. This is only another way of saying that infinitives and participles cannot be predicates. *I buying my books* is not a sentence, for there is not a complete thought. There is a subject, *I*, but no predicate. When we hear the words, *A gentleman walking along the street*, we wait, expecting to hear more : the gentleman must fall, or get run over, or enter a shop—he must do something before we are satisfied.

A group of words without a finite part of a verb forms not a sentence, but a phrase; the words make sense, but not complete sense. Here, for instance, are phrases that yield a certain sense :—

Being unable to stifle his remorse . . .
To have worked well . . .
For the good of the State . . .

To turn them into sentences, we must add the finite part of some verb, thus :—

Being unable to stifle his remorse, he shot himself.

To have worked well is small satisfaction.

For the good of the State they are willing to sacrifice their happiness and their liberty.

Exercise 4

(*a*) Change the following phrases into sentences by adding some statement containing a finite part of a verb at the place where the dash occurs :—

1. Notwithstanding all he had undergone —— 2. —— after having done his utmost. 3. Proceeding up the dangerous defile ——. 4. ——

to have accosted him. 5. —— to know a little of everything. 6. After reposing some hours in the hut of a peasant —— 7. Puffed into existence by unscrupulous speculators —— 8. —— even by the appointment of a regular wit. 9. Frederick, without a guinea in his pocket, and having left not many in the pockets of his friends —— 10. —— to fall at once from the pinnacle of neglect.

(b) Make simple sentences introducing the three words given :—

    (i) Cuckoo—south—nest.
   (ii) Clock—hour—chime.
  (iii) Silver—light—candles.

LESSON V

THE SENTENCE—ORDER OF WORDS

The natural order of words in a sentence is : Subject—verb—object. In some cases no other order is possible. *William defeated Harold* is the only way in which we can state the fact while restricting ourselves to these three words. *Harold defeated William* is untrue. *William Harold defeated* and *Harold William defeated* are not only clumsy forms, but they leave it doubtful which of the two was defeated. *Defeated William Harold* is nonsense. Here, then, no other order is permissible than subject—verb—object.

With *William defeated him* we can take more liberties. *Him William defeated* is as clear as the regular form, though we feel that it is less natural. Even the form *Him defeated William* is intelligible, though unjustifiable.

When a sentence contains more words than the bare three necessary to give subject, verb and object still greater freedom may be allowed. The following sentence from Gray's *Elegy* keeps the normal word-order : *The ploughman homeward plods his weary way*, but it is possible to express in a great many ways without materially altering the meaning. Here are some of the more obvious :—

Homeward the ploughman plods his weary way.

His weary way the ploughman plods homeward.

Plods the ploughman his weary way homeward.

Homeward his weary way plods the ploughman.

His weary way the ploughman homeward plods.

Plods homeward the ploughman his weary way.

The ploughman plods his weary way homeward.

We might strain ingenuity still further by producing still more forms of the same sentence, but they would soon become not only unnatural, but almost unintelligible. They merely afford an example of the way in which word-order may vary. You may ask, indeed, why we should trouble to vary the order when the normal order is clear. Certainly on most occasions the normal order is to be preferred, but there are times when we must change it in order to make certain parts of the sentence more emphatic, or to gain variety.

It is found that the beginning and the end of a sentence are the important places for catching the attention of the reader. These places accordingly give greater emphasis to any words that are placed there. You have only to read over the different arrangements of Gray's sentence to see the truth of this. Every one of the variations conveys a slightly different meaning because the emphasis falls on different ideas. All the sentences convey the general meaning that a wearied ploughman is plodding his way home; but some of them make us think more of the ploughman, others more of the plodding, other again more of the home or of the weariness. The truth is that while, *for all practical purposes*, the same idea may be expressed by two or more forms of the same sentence, there is only *one* form for the *exact* expression of any given idea.

Since the beginning and the end of a sentence are the emphatic places, we easily understand why little, insignificant words should not be placed in these positions of advantage. It is sometimes said that words should be arranged in a sentence as officers used to arrange their men in the old hand-to-hand fighting days—the big ones in the front and rear, the little ones in the middle. There is this difference, however, that while in fighting the van is more important than the rear, the end of the sentence is, on the whole, more important than the beginning. It used to be given as an absolute rule that no sentence should ever begin with *And* or *But*. This rule is now not insisted on, though it is not desirable to have many sentences beginning with these. A sentence should begin and end as well as we can make it, but if one of the two must suffer, let it not be the ending. Prepositions, pronouns, small unemphatic adverbs and adjectives are endings to be avoided. A weak ending is sometimes produced by the use of a passive form, and where this happens we should turn the sentence into the active, as in the first and the last sentences given below.

Bad.	Not so Bad.
Games and other forms of amusement were indulged in.	They indulged in games and other forms of amusement.
We have no chance of learning since everything is done for us.	Since everything is done for us we have no chance of learning.
He paid all his debts to the amount of three thousand pounds then.	Then he paid . . . [if we wish to emphasise the time], or, He paid then all his debts to the amount of three thousand pounds.
Houses and lands were things he had quite lost the desire of.	He had quite lost the desire of houses and lands.

This desire to have something solid to rest on at the end of a sentence depends largely upon the ear, and may be illustrated by reference to music. Not every note of the scale can make a satisfactory ending : there are certain notes that make natural halting-places, and certain others which the ear declines to accept as final.

Exercise 5

(a) Write out the following sentence in as many different arrangements as you can with-

43

out making it lose its general sense. Number your versions in order, beginning with the version that you think the most satisfactory :—

We came to our journey's end, at last, with no small difficulty, after much fatigue, through deep roads, and bad weather.

(*b*) Write a short account (about a hundred words) of a walk in the country, such as you might write in a diary. (Describe the way you went, where you had tea, how you came back, anything of interest you saw.) Use simple sentences as far as possible.

LESSON VI

THE SENTENCE—KINDS OF SIMPLE SENTENCES

The second cause which leads to variation from the natural order of subject—verb—object is the desire to avoid monotony. A page or two of direct statements of the Cows-eat-grass type would be intolerable in a book meant for general reading. In legal documents, and in business papers generally, it is often necessary to gain clearness and save time even at the expense of monotony. But in what is usually called composition a certain amount of variety is necessary.

Even the most simple sentences need not be always expressed in the standard form, so long as the change involves no loss of clearness. Those that we have hitherto dealt with have made plain, straightforward statements. Such a sentence is, *None of the soldiers was dismayed.*

But the same idea may be expressed in the

interrogative form, as Tennyson puts it : *Was there a man dismayed?* Though this is put in the form of a question, Tennyson did not want an answer. It is what is called a rhetorical question. An orator or preacher often goes on asking questions which he would be greatly surprised if any one answered. The answer is supposed to be implied in the very nature of things. The question is, in fact, an exclamation. Sometimes, indeed, there is a difficulty in saying whether a sentence which is interrogative in form should have the question mark (?) or the exclamation mark (!) after it. In : *Who can number the stars of the firmament,* we may use either *!* or *?*

Then we have sentences which express a wish. *God speed the right. May your shadow never grow less.* Finally, we have sentences in which an order or an authoritative piece of advice is given. *Charge for the guns. Never use a big word when a little one will do as well.*

With these five kinds of simple sentences we have ample scope for variety of form. But we must not forget that the ordinary straightforward form of the sentence should always be preferred, unless there is some reason for departing from it. There is a style of writing that seeks to gain brightness by twisting the words of the sentence into unnatural positions. *Go downstairs I could not* may be passed if found as one example of inversion in a passage, particularly if the tone of the passage is somewhat elevated. But for an ordinary construction such a sentence is to be condemned.

You must note that while the following exercise gives practice in changing the form of sentences, it does not at all follow that the change is for the better. So long as wearisome monotony is avoided, the more direct you can make your sentences the better.

Exercise 6

Change the following into the interrogative form without materially altering the meaning :—

(a) 1. This is not English straightforwardness. 2. A braver man is not to be found. 3. There is no longer any doubt about the matter. 4. There is not a scrap of evidence against him. 5. I am no dog that I should do this thing.

Change the following into the exclamatory form without materially altering the meaning :—

(b) 1. He has a very ugly mouth. 2. I dislike babies very much. 3. The ways of God are wonderful. 4. There is plenty of plunder here.

(c) Write a short description of waking up on a snowy morning, using the following notes as a guide, if you are at a loss what to say :—

On waking, the lightness of the room—the stillness outside—footmarks in the snowy street—snow falling again—men sweeping the snow away—difference between snow in town and snow in the country.

LESSON VII

THE SENTENCE—COMPOUND AND COMPLEX SENTENCES

When a sentence contains only one subject and one predicate it is called a simple sentence. All the sentences we have hitherto considered are simple sentences. But sentences frequently contain several subjects and predicates. When two simple sentences are joined together we have a new sentence with two subjects and two predicates. Consider these two simple sentences :—

The Spaniard swerved aside. The dagger grazed his ear.

These can be combined in several ways, as thus :—

The Spaniard swerved aside and the dagger grazed his ear.
The Spaniard swerved aside : the dagger grazed his ear.

In both cases two simple sentences have been rolled into one : in the first they are linked by the conjunction, *and* ; in the second the conjunction has been replaced by a colon. When two sentences are thus combined, they cease to be called sentences, and, in relation to the new sentence which they form, they are called *Clauses*. In these sentences both clauses are equally important, and neither is dependent on the other. A sentence formed from such clauses is called a *Compound Sentence*. There may be any number of clauses in a Compound Sentence, provided each is independent, e.g. *The cat mewed, the dog whined, and the baby howled for its rattle*.

Sometimes the clauses are not independent. Examine the following sentences :—

1. *Here is a portrait of my grandmother, who was in her youth a very beautiful woman*. Here the clause *who was a very beautiful woman* is dependent on the first clause. Its purpose is to describe *my grandmother*, so that it really stands in place of an adjective.

2. *The seal was discovered where it had fallen.*
Here the clause expands what the verb tells us,
and really stands in place of an adverb.

3. *He told the cook that the house was on fire.*
Here the clause stands for what he told the cook,
and might be replaced by a noun such as *news*.
It is the object of the verb *told*, and stands in
place of a noun.

In all these cases we have a principal clause
and a subordinate one, the whole sentence being
called *Complex*. There is no limit to the number
of subordinate clauses that may be found in a
complex sentence. We may have all three
kinds present in the same sentence. *When
Edward learned the true state of affairs, he decided
that the hostages who had been sent should be at once
executed.* The relation of the clauses in this
sentence is more clearly seen if we set them out
like a family tree :—

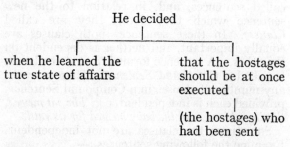

He decided

when he learned the
true state of affairs

that the hostages
should be at once
executed

(the hostages) who
had been sent

We can also have sentences which are both complex and compound. These contain two principal clauses and one or more dependent clauses,
as : *They reached the battlements which were
deserted by the sentinels, and put the entire garrison
to the sword.*

For the purposes of composition the triple classification is sufficient—simple sentences : compound sentences (*i.e.*, those having two or more principal clauses but no subordinate clauses) : and complex sentences (*i.e.*, those having one or more principal, and one or more subordinate clauses). Compare the following example : the principal verbs are in bold type :—

John Gilpin **was** a citizen of credit and renown.
Simple.

The Queen of France, being a Spaniard, would not, he **thought,** be welcome. Complex.

Tom **put** out his pink palm, and Bob **was** not slow to place his hard, grimy hand within it.
Compound.

You must be on your guard against the error of regarding the grammatical principal clause as really the most important clause. *He told me that my house had been burned to the ground. He told* is grammatically the principal clause, but the subordinate noun clause would be the important one for me. What does it matter who told me, compared with the fact that my house is ruined ? On the other hand, if the news were false, and the question was who had spread the disagreeable story, the grammatical principal clause would also be the really important one.

Exercise 7

(*a*) In the following sentences underline the principal (grammatical) verb or verbs, and set them out in such a way as to show the relation of the clauses (as in the example on p. 48).

1. There's a story that when the mill changes

hands, the river's angry. 2. Nevertheless we have reason to be thankful that the thing, well or ill, is over. 3. Love heaven; let your heart be on it. 4. I could easily give you more definite, but very disagreeable proofs of the evil of knowing the anatomy of the human face too intimately.

(b) Combine the simple sentences of your account of a country walk into longer sentences.

(c) Do the same in the passage given on p. 189.

LESSON VIII

THE SENTENCE—KINDS OF COMPOUND SENTENCES

When simple sentences are joined together to make compound sentences, the combination may be effected in different ways. First, the two parts may be of equal importance and of the same character. They may be joined by a conjunction : *The mate opened his mouth, and the pipe fell from it* ; or they may have only a colon between them : *Fox went into Parliament at twenty : Pitt when just of age.* Or one part of the sentence may be opposed to or contrasted with the other. *Acids turn litmus red, but alkalies turn it blue.* Speaking generally, the conjunction *and* is the mark of the first kind of sentence, the conjunction *but* of the second. But the meaning alone can determine the relation between the clauses. *Lord Bruce was made an earl for a blunder in prosody : and Nelson was made a baron for the victory of the Nile.* Here the clauses are clearly contrasted, though joined by *and*. If Pitt had been old when he entered Parliament, the clauses of the sentence above would become contrasted, though the form remained unchanged.

The two clauses may be separated from one another as alternatives, or plainly disjoined from each other : *She must weep or she will die. You will neither use the material yourself nor allow others to do so.*

Again, the two clauses may be so related that one of them gives the cause of what is stated in the other : *The King had abdicated : therefore Henry's course was clear.*

In the examples given above both subjects and both predicates are expressed, but it frequently happens that one verb has to do duty for several subjects, and as frequently one subject has several verbs. *The populace, the patricians, the Emperor himself yielded to the impulse of the moment. The interloper fawned, flattered, yet failed.* Each of these two compound sentences is made up of three simple sentences.

In the first case we have three sentences with the same predicate :—

The populace yielded to the impulse of the moment.
The patricians yielded to the impulse of the moment.
The Emperor himself yielded to the impulse of the moment.

In the second case we have three sentences with the same subject :—

The interloper fawned.
The interloper flattered.
The interloper failed.

Exercise 8

(*a*) Complete the following sentences :—

1. Such treatment I did not expect, for —— 2. Sir, you are either ignorant or —— 3. Cain as well as Abel —— 4. The table was literally loaded with good cheer, and —— 5. Man proposes —— 6. —— in consequence the work had to be re-written. 7. —— but his pleadings were in vain. 8. —— and ready to forgive. 9. This made Christian give a little back; Apollyon therefore —— 10. He shuddered; he grew pale; he —— 11. —— accordingly Wellington gave it an emphatic denial. 12. Forster counterfeits a passion too, but ——

(*b*) Turn the simple sentences in your description of a snowy morning into longer sentences by turning them into complex or compound sentences.

(*c*) Do the same for the passage given on p. 190.

LESSON IX

THE SENTENCE—RELATIVE CLAUSES

Simple sentences are often rolled into one with the help of a relative clause.

He supports his mother.   She has bad health.

These sentences in combination become :—

He supports his mother who has bad health.

This is the just and proper use of the relative. It should not, however, be used where it is possible to use an adjective or participle instead.

If we wish to roll the following sentences into one, we should do so by transferring the adjective :—

He supports his mother.   She is an invalid.
He supports his invalid mother.

The next can be linked by a participle in the same way :—

Sir William has a favourite dog.   Its name is Diamond.
Sir William has a favourite dog named Diamond.

These copulative relative clauses, as they are called, should always be used in moderation; they are clumsy and unwieldy when used in excess.   They are most abused when they are hitched one behind another, like a train of carriages behind a railway engine.   The classic example of this chain construction is the nursery rhyme, " The House that Jack Built," but it is found also in serious prose, as, for example :—

" Sir William used to show with pride a silver casket which he had received from an Indian prince whom he had been able to accommodate in a small matter which had arisen out of the diplomatic entanglements which necessarily arise in countries which are broken up into petty states, whose rulers are kept at peace only by fear of the force which the Government can bring to bear upon those princes who transgress the limits which it marks out."

In this monstrous sentence, nine simple sentences have been tacked together, and the connection between the first and the last is remote in the extreme.

There is another use of the relative clause that must be distinguished from that we have illustrated. *The soul that sinneth shall die.* In this case we cannot split the sentence up into two independent sentences. *The soul shall die* is complete so far as it goes. But it is not true as it stands. We are not told that the soul in general shall die, but only a particular kind of soul, the kind that sins. In other words, the relative clause *that sinneth* really limits the meaning of the whole sentence. This is called the restrictive use of the relative; the other kind illustrates what may be called the copulative or co-ordinative use. Generally speaking, the restrictive use prefers *that*, while the copulative use prefers *who* or *which*. But this cannot be depended on in discriminating the two. It is carrying criticism too far to ask a Scotsman to change his patriotic song from *Scots wha hae* to *Scots that hae*. The rule, in fact, is not rigid, as is seen in Ruskin's : " The man who does not know when to die, does not know how to live ". We should in most cases use *that* in restrictive clauses, but we need not bind ourselves to the one form. Sometimes the flow of the sentence is improved by a *who* or *which*.

The best way of discriminating between the two uses is to note whether the relative clause is in any way parenthetic. Try if the main sentence can stand quite alone, and mean exactly the same thing, *so far as it goes*, after we have taken away the relative clause. *The man who writes for fools is always sure of a large audience.* Here, if we cut out *who writes for fools* we take away the whole point of the sentence. The real subject is not *man* but man-who-writes-for-fools.

In the sentence, *That man, who is talking to the porter, is her brother,* we find that the relative clause tells us more about *that man* than is found in the main clause, but does not materially affect the main clause.

In the copulative or co-ordinative use of the relative it is found that *who* and *which* are practically equal to *and he* (or *she*) *and it.* *My father, whom I left at home, will be here presently* really equals *My father* (*and I left him at home*) *will be here presently.* But *The friend that I left at home will be here presently* cannot be separated in this way.

Students who are studying, or intend to study, French or Latin should attend specially to this distinction between restrictive and copulative relative clauses.

Exercise 9

(*a*) Combine the following sets of simple sentences into complex sentences; first with a restrictive relative clause, and secondly with a copulative relative clause, in each case :—

1. The man was exempted from military service. His mother was a widow. 2. The ship was built by Jackson & Co. It was wrecked. 3. Mary had a little lamb. It went with her to school. 4. The novelist has few friends. He is despised. He is conceited.

(*b*) Break up the sentence about Sir William (on p. 53) into simple sentences, and then combine them into sentences of suitable length.

LESSON X

THE SENTENCE—LOOSE AND PERIODIC SENTENCES

There are said to be two great classes of sentences according to the general principles on which they are constructed. There is first the **loose** sentence. Its characteristic is that it puts the main idea of the sentence in the front, and adds piecemeal whatever is thought necessary. In this form of sentence the author is tempted to add fact after fact as they occur to him, and as they all have some sort of connection with the main idea, they may fairly be included in the same sentence, though the looseness of the connection is often apparent enough to justify the name. The first sentence of *Robinson Crusoe* supplies an excellent example.

"I was born in the year 1632, in the city of York, of a good family, though not of that country, my father being a foreigner of Bremen, who settled first at Hull : he got a good estate by merchandise, and leaving off his trade, lived afterward at York, from whence he had married my mother, whose relations were named Robinson, a very good family in that country, and from whom I was called Robinson Kreutznaer; but, by the usual corruption of words in England, we are now called, nay, we call ourselves, and write our name Crusoe, and so my companions always called me."

Defoe is here writing in a conversational manner. He seems to lengthen his sentence as the facts occur to him, and there seems no reason why it should ever come to end. This kind of sentence is very appropriate to informal writing, especially where the first person is used.

The other kind of sentence, known as the **periodic,** arranges for a termination by keeping the principal statement to the end. In Dr. Johnson we find :—

" If, therefore, he whose crimes have deprived him of the favour of God can reflect upon his conduct without disturbance, or can at will banish the reflection ; if he who considers himself as suspended over the abyss of eternal perdition only by the thread of life, which must soon part by its own weakness, and which the wing of every minute may divide, can cast his eyes round him without shuddering with horror or panting with security, what can he judge of himself but that he is not yet awakened to sufficient conviction ? "

The name *periodic* is apt to convey the impression that this sort of sentence must be long, and generally speaking the impression is correct. But the real test is not the length of the whole sentence, but the place of the principal idea at the end rather than at the beginning.

After the most straitest sect of our religion I lived a Pharisee is periodic ; *I lived a Pharisee after the most straitest sect of our religion* is loose.

A very common kind of periodic sentence begins with clauses preceded by *that*.

" That the life and progress on which he built such hopes, should be endangered in the outset by so mean a want : that Dombey and Son should be tottering for a nurse, was a sore humiliation."

It is not to be supposed that all sentences obligingly fall into the two classes : those that begin with the main idea, and those that end with it. In many cases the main idea comes about the middle, as in the following sentences quoted from Charles Lamb :—

" With great deference to the old lady's judgment in these matters, I think I have experienced some moments in my life, when playing at cards for nothing has even been agreeable. When I am in sickness, or not in the best of spirits, I sometimes call for the cards, and play a game at piquet for love with my cousin Bridget—Bridget Elia."

These seem to be neither loose nor periodic, but those who lay great store upon exact definitions will be glad to learn that all sentences that do not begin with the main statement are called periodic, so that the sentences just quoted are technically known as periodic sentences. The original sentence given in Exercise 5 is loose. All the variations on it are periodic.

The very name " loose " is sufficient to prejudice the unwary against the first kind of sentence. Almost invariably a student when asked which is the better form of sentence answers, " The periodic ". The answer should be, " It depends upon the connection in which it is used ". In speaking, as opposed to writing, the loose construction is frequently to be preferred. If the hearer knows what the sentence is about in general terms, he can examine each new statement as it is presented : but if all the subordinate clauses come first, he cannot understand their bearing, and is very apt to get tired and give up attending before the explanatory ending is reached. "That St. Paul was struck blind at Damascus, that he had to gaze steadfastly in order to distinguish the High Priest, that he wrote to the Galatians in large characters, that these same Galatians were at one time willing to give even their own eyes for him, all lead us to believe that St. Paul's ' thorn in the flesh ' consisted in a weakness of the eyes."

Such a sentence demands a second reading; for the first four clauses cannot be estimated as arguments till it is known what position they are used to establish. In a speech the sentence is bad; in a written argument it is quite permissible. It cannot be too strongly impressed upon writers and speakers that it is not enough that they should so express themselves that any one who cares to take pains can understand what they write or speak : the ideal is to express oneself so that hearers or readers cannot help understanding.

The true view is that both loose and periodic sentences ought to be used in all kinds of composition, but that in speaking the loose should predominate, and in writing the periodic. It has been made clear already that a periodic sentence is not necessarily either long or heavy. *Reduced to his last cartridge he fired it and fell* is regarded by some authorities as a more finished sentence than *He fell after he had fired his last cartridge*. But there is not difference enough to quarrel over. The important thing is to use both forms in a composition, so that monotony of structure may be avoided.

Exercise 10

(a) State in the case of each of the following eight sentences whether it is loose or periodic : if it is loose turn it into the periodic form, if it is periodic then change it to the loose form.

1. When Edward the Black Prince made your king his prisoner, he reverenced his age, his station, his misfortunes; attending him, serving him, consoling him, like a son. 2. He would, as became him, have kept behind his master, if the knight had not called him to his side, complaining that the length and roughness of the roads had shaken his saddle so as to make it uneven and uneasy. 3. Among the beautiful and simple-hearted customs of rural life which still linger in some parts of England, are those of strewing flowers before the funerals, and planting them at the graves of departed friends. 4. There is something genuine and affectionate in the gaiety of the young, when it is excited by the bounty and familiarity of their elders. 5. The simple truth is that the Aristotelians erected their castles upon a basis far less reliable than air. 6. In attempting to appreciate this interval by the aid of any considerations of velocity, as we did in endeavouring to estimate the distance of the moon, we must leave out of sight altogether such nothings as the speed of a cannon ball or of sound. 7. If any pretend that they have the Spirit, and so turn away from the straight rule of the Holy Scriptures, they have a spirit indeed, but it is a fanatical spirit, the spirit of delusion and giddiness. 8. From the circumstance of the dinner being composed of pig's head mock-turtle soup, of pig's fry and roast

ribs of pork, I am led to imagine that one of Ponto's black Hampshires had been sacrificed a short time before my visit.

(*b*) Make up a loose sentence on the pleasures of living in a city, and a periodic sentence on the pleasures of living in the country.

LESSON XI

THE SENTENCE—LENGTH AND BALANCE OF SENTENCES

The claims of long and short sentences must be treated in exactly the same way as we have treated those of loose and periodic sentences. There is room in composition for both : each in its own place is best. They ought to be used together ; the one kind acts as a foil to the other. A passage written entirely in very short sentences lacks dignity and weight : it conveys the impression of being very brittle and ready to fall to pieces : it is jerky, and gives no resting-places for the mind. On the other hand, long sentences, such as Johnson sometimes uses, are exceedingly cumbrous, and make an unnecessarily heavy demand on our attention. It is true that many of those long sentences are not sentences at all, since they are merely several sentences joined together by semicolons, instead of being separated by periods. They are really paragraphs.

The short sentence must, on the whole, have the preference. Wherever there is any doubt, always decide for the shorter sentence. But it is well to recognise that the long sentence has its place and use. Short sentences are very useful to introduce a general principle which is to be elaborated. Somewhat longer sentences are useful in working out the principle. Shorter sentences are again useful in gathering up conclusions drawn from the treatment of a subject.

Different kinds of writing demand different lengths of sentence. Description usually permits of pretty equal proportions of long and short; argument often requires a preponderance of long sentences; narrative generally prefers the short sentence. Especially in the case of rapid action the short sentence is useful. Thus, in telling how Crusoe prepared to meet the savages, Defoe says :—

" I turned to Friday. ' Now, Friday,' said I, ' do as I bid thee.' Friday said he would. ' Then, Friday,' says I, ' do exactly as you see me do—fail in nothing.' "

This is followed by longer sentences describing how things were done : the dramatic short sentence is no longer needed. Apart from this need for variety in length, the short sentence justifies its existence because it tends, on the whole, to greater clearness.[1]

We have seen that neither the loose nor the periodic form is necessarily long : but the loose sentence has a natural tendency to swell beyond its legitimate size. When once the main idea has been expressed, the way seems so clear for less important matter that we are tempted to go

---

[1] Of modern writers, Ernest Hemingway shows marked preference for short sentences, and uses them with great effect.

on adding clause after clause till the sentence becomes monstrous. To a certain extent the subordinate matters are kept in their place, since they follow the main statement. But there are degrees of subordination, and the less important clauses should be so arranged as to indicate the greater or less importance of each. The loose sentence tempts us to put them down in the mere order in which they occur to us.

Try to complete every sentence in your mind before setting it down on paper. This does not mean that you are to sit mouthing over every word in a sentence before you write it down : but it does mean that you must know the exact kind of sentence you are dealing with, and its exact scope. Afterthoughts in the middle of a sentence often cause what is called a broken construction (see p. 121), and almost always cause an unpleasant lopsidedness in sentences. Clearly the loose sentence is more liable to abuse in this way than is the periodic. From the very beginning the important point of the periodic sentence must be kept in view : we are working up to that main point, and are therefore not likely to let too many smaller ideas come between us and our goal. In the loose sentence we can make a beginning and go on without having well considered the end. In the periodic, the end must be clearly conceived from the very beginning.

In sentence-building the matter of balance is too often neglected. Wherever possible the parts should be so arranged that each supports the others, and that similar parts are grouped together, and dissimilar parts contrasted with each other. A sentence, for example, may contain three principal clauses, the first with one subordinate clause, the second with three, the last with none. Here we have a clear case of lack of balance. The sentence is lopsided. We must not, however, go to the opposite extreme, and arrange that each of the clauses shall have three subordinate clauses, whether the meaning demands it or not. Nothing can justify the padding out of sentences when the meaning is clear enough already.

" The tower was captured in spite of all the villagers could do, the baron was killed in the very room in which he had caused Gerald to be put to death because of his refusal to sign the declaration when the first troop of insurgents had arrived in defiance of the orders the cardinal had issued, and Fenton had to seek a new master."

The sentence is so lopsided as to be unpleasant, but the remedy is not to be sought in adding balancing clauses at the beginning and the end. The whole requires to be recast. Take the following sentence from Gibbon, and you cannot fail to find satisfaction in the balance of the two final clauses.

" The unsuccessful expedition of Hannibal served only to display the character of the senate and people; of a senate degraded, rather than ennobled, by the comparison of an assembly of kings; and of a people to whom the ambassador of Pyrrhus ascribed the inexhaustible resources of the Hydra."

It is generally supposed that the periodic sentence lends itself more readily than the loose to this just balancing; but the sentence quoted is loose and yet perfectly balanced.

Johnson is noted for his balanced sentences. Indeed, he cannot be regarded as quite guiltless of sacrificing matter to style in the rounding of his periods. The following is an excellent example of a Johnsonian sentence :—

" The power of invention has been conferred by nature upon few, and the labour of learning those sciences which may by mere labour be obtained, is too great to be willingly endured; but every man can exert such judgment as he has upon the works of others; and he whom nature has made weak, and idleness keeps ignorant, may yet support his vanity by the name of a critic."

There is first the general balance of the part that precedes and the part that follows the first semicolon. Then there is the balance of the two main clauses that make up the second part. Finally, there is the balance of the two subordinate clauses contained in the final main clause.

This may be called the double or two-pulse balance, but Johnson is very fond of the three-pulse or triple balance. It has been sarcastically said that each of Johnson's essays could be made into three essays by simply selecting, one after the other, the first, the second and the third of his balanced nouns, adjectives and verbs. Most people would be content with saying that at certain periods the world is filled with bloodshed. Johnson makes it filled with " ravage, bloodshed and devastation ".

" Men then grow weary of debate and altercation, and apply themselves to the arts of profit : trading companies are formed, manufactures improved, and navigation extended; and nothing is any longer thought on but the increase and preservation of property, the artifices of getting money, and the pleasures of spending it."

Here the whole sentence, as separated by the semicolons, represents the triple balance, each of the three parts having a subordinate balance of its own; the first subordinate balance is double, the next two triple.

This poised style, though it can be applied to both the loose and the periodic sentence, is generally known as the periodic style. It is no longer popular, which is not altogether to be regretted, as it formed a strong temptation to subordinate thought to expression. Nature has not arranged that things shall fall into well-ordered groups of pairs and elegant series of trilogies to suit the convenience of the writer of periods. But the reaction goes too far. Our ordinary style pays too little heed to the flow of words. Our sentences are often so short that we feel as if our minds were jolted from one idea to the other. More frequently our longer sentences are mere huddles of clauses, badly joined together or not joined at all.

" It ought to be presumed that a publisher who conducts a respectable and honourable business will, when he retires from it, probably do so, however suddenly, respectably and honourably; and he ought not to be deprived of the right, which he himself allows the author, of assigning his interest in the work if necessary."

Here we have neither balance nor flow. Ask any one to read the sentence aloud, and you will find how essentially bad it is. *This test of reading aloud ought to be applied to all the sentences that you write by way of practice.* It is not meant that prose should flow as smoothly as verse, but it should flow; it should not be a series of gasps or pistol shots. The sentence quoted gasps along in puffs, till it comes to *suddenly* : there, where it ought to halt, it begins to flow. *Suddenly, respectably and honourably* run into one another with an ease that is as vicious as is the preceding stiffness.

Exercise II

(*a*) Re-cast the first half of the sentence about the publisher.

(*b*) Throw the whole of the Crusoe sentences into one.

(*c*) The following passage is taken from *Pickwick Papers.* Bob Sawyer is giving a party, and his friend Jack Hopkins is telling Mr. Pickwick a very tall story about his experiences as a medical student. Re-write the story as it might appear in a daily paper, leaving out all unnecessary details (the conversation, the shoulder of mutton, etc.). Make the account as dramatic as possible, using longer sentences for the plainer parts of the narrative, short sentences for the exciting parts.

" By the bye," said Hopkins, ". . . we had a curious accident last night. A child was brought in, who had swallowed a necklace."

" Swallowed what, sir ? " interrupted Mr. Pickwick.

" A necklace," replied Jack Hopkins. " Not all at once, you know, that would be too much. . . . No, the way was this. Child's parents

were poor people who lived in a court. Child's
eldest sister bought a necklace; common necklace, made of large wooden beads. Child, being
fond of toys, cribbed the necklace, hid it, played
with it, cut the string, swallowed a bead. Child
thought it capital fun, went back next day,
swallowed another bead."

"Bless my heart," said Mr. Pickwick, "what
a dreadful thing! I beg your pardon, sir. Go
on."

"Next day, child swallowed two beads; the
day after that, he treated himself to three, and
so on, till in a week's time he had got through the
necklace—five and twenty beads in all. The
sister . . . cried her eyes out at the loss of the
necklace; looked high and low for it; but, I
needn't say, didn't find it. A few days afterwards, the family were at dinner—baked shoulder
of mutton, and potatoes under it—the child, who
wasn't hungry, was playing about the room, when
suddenly there was heard a devil of a noise, like
a small hailstorm. 'Don't do that, my boy,' said
the father. 'I ain't doin' nothing,' said the
child. 'Well, don't do it again,' said the father.
There was a short silence, and then the noise
began again, worse than ever. 'If you don't
mind what I say, my boy,' said the father,
'you'll find yourself in bed in something less than
a pig's whisper.' He gave the child a shake to
make him obedient, and such a rattling ensued as
nobody ever heard before. 'Why, damme, it's
in the child!' said the father, 'he's got croup in
the wrong place!' 'No, I haven't, father,' said
the child, beginning to cry, 'it's the necklace; I
swallowed it, father.'—The father caught the
child up and ran with him to the hospital, the

beads in the boy's stomach rattling all the way with the jolting, and the people looking up in the air, and down in the cellars to see where the unusual noise came from. He's in the hospital now," said Jack Hopkins, " and he makes such a devil of a noise when he walks about, that they're obliged to muffle him in a watchman's coat, for fear he should wake the patients !"

(*Note.*—Your own version should be about two-thirds the length of the original.)

LESSON XII

THE PARAGRAPH

The paragraph bears the same relation to an essay, an article or a chapter that the sentence does to the paragraph. The sentence is often said to be " complete in itself ", but in many cases this is true only in a grammatical sense. Take the isolated sentences given in the exercises of this book, and you cannot fail to see how incomplete they are as they stand. There is the proper number of verbs and subjects : all the grammatical rules have been attended to : yet we feel that in many cases we cannot be quite sure about the real meaning. When several sentences have been so grouped as to explain each other, and together make up a more or less independent part of a longer composition, they form a paragraph.

A great many of the points dealt with regarding sentences have to be considered in connection

c

with paragraphs. To begin with, a paragraph has only a modified independence. It must depend upon the other paragraphs for its full meaning. If this is not so, it is not a paragraph, but a little essay by itself.

Next comes the question whether paragraphs should be long or short. Here we must be guided by the same principles that we applied to sentences. If we are dealing with events rapidly taking place we must have short paragraphs. In ordinary descriptive or argumentative work they ought to be longer. The modern tendency is to shorten the paragraph unduly. A page of solid printing is almost as distasteful to the public as to the compositor. The very same matter that repels when presented in a block, seems attractive when broken up into four or five portions. Within limits the tendency to shorten paragraphs is to be encouraged. To feel that you must say all that you have to say on each aspect of your subject in the fewest possible sentences has a wholesome effect. One danger is that the thought expressed in paragraphs may become unduly compressed. The more serious danger is that short paragraphs are made by the simple process of cutting up a long paragraph into bits of the required length. The resulting groups of sentences are no longer paragraphs in any respect but appearance. In consequence of this mechanical shortening of paragraphs many modern books have a very spasmodic, jerky style that interferes with the flow of thought. The following illustrates the jerky effect of too short paragraphs :—

" Let me face it quietly. To-day I am actually beset with a fresh disaster and a worse one.

" ' You are a pauper, Archibald Seaton.'

" This is what the city roared to me an hour or two ago.

" The simple story of a stupid investor once again.

" When I married I wanted my income stretched to its utmost extent, and against the advice of the family solicitor invested all *The Demon* does not claim in the Del Norte Gold Mines, then paying 10 per cent.

" An old Oxford acquaintance of Hebrew extraction, who had adopted the name of an ancient Scotch family, tempted me, and I fell.

" For two years the dividends were paid. Yesterday the company went into liquidation, and my few poor thousands have vanished into thin air like a ghost in Virgil.

" In the City, where I ran like a frightened rabbit, I met fellow-shareholders in a similar plight—a white-faced, panic-stricken crew.

" To me there is a certain grim humour in the situation.

" I distinctly hear two voices.

" My Uncle Linton is saying, ' That unlucky ass, Archibald ! ' My father-in-law is rubbing the back of his left hand with the palm of his right, exclaiming to Christabel, ' What a calamity ! What a calamity ! How is it he never consulted me ? Was ever any one so unbusinesslike ? ' And what is my wife saying ? She, I know, will say nothing—only wonder silently how we are to live.

" And how do I feel ? Much like a sentient cork drifting with the blind black tide of disaster."

Even in verse, where the stanza forms the

natural paragraph, we find that poets are frequently compelled to carry on the thought of one stanza into the next, and to do this have sometimes to split a sentence between the stanzas. The truth is that paragraphs must vary in length according to the requirements of each case, exactly as do sentences. The tendency should always be towards shortness.

As to the arrangement of sentences in a paragraph, no hard and fast rules can be laid down. It is generally more effective to begin and end with shorter sentences, while the middle is occupied with those of more complicated construction. In an essay the shorter sentences introduce clearly and boldly the argument of the paragraph, the longer sentences unfold it, and the short closing sentences gather up and clinch what has gone before. In a descriptive paragraph the same process is very often followed. Here is a simple, yet effective, paragraph from Cowper's letters :—

"I have a kitten, my dearest Cousin, the drollest of all creatures that ever wore a cat's skin. Her gambols are not to be described, and would be incredible, if they could. In point of size she is likely to be a kitten always, being extremely small of her age, but time, I suppose, that spoils everything, will make her also a cat. You will see her, I hope, before that melancholy period shall arrive, for no wisdom that she may gain by experience and reflection hereafter, will compensate the loss of her present hilarity. She is dressed in a tortoise-shell suit, and I know that you will delight in her."

Exercise 12

(*a*) The following passage from Lamb's essay, " Mrs. Battle's Opinions on Whist ", is divided in the original into four paragraphs. Read it over carefully and try to discover where each new paragraph begins.

" ' A clear fire, a clean hearth, and the rigour of the game.' This was the celebrated *wish* of old Sarah Battle (now with God) who, next to her devotions, loved a good game at whist. She was none of your lukewarm gamesters, your half and half players, who have no objection to take a hand, if you want one to make up a rubber; who affirm they have no pleasure in winning; that they like to win one game and lose another; that they can while away an hour very agreeably at a card table, but are indifferent whether they play or no; and will desire an adversary, who has slipt a wrong card, to take it up and play another. These insufferable triflers are the curse of a table. One of these flies will spoil a whole pot. Of such may it be said, that they do not play at cards, but only play at playing at them. Sarah Battle was none of that breed. She detested them, as I do, from her heart and soul; and would not, save upon a striking emergency, willingly seat herself at the same table with them. She loved a thorough-paced partner, a determined enemy. She took, and gave, no concessions. She hated favours. She fought a good fight : cut and thrust. She held not her good sword (her cards) ' like a dancer '. She sat bolt upright; and neither showed you her cards, nor desired to see yours.

All people have their blind side—their superstitions; and I have heard her declare, under the
rose, that Hearts was her favourite suit. I
never in my life—and I knew Sarah Battle
many of the best years of it—saw her take out
her snuff-box when it was her turn to play; or
snuff a candle in the middle of a game; or ring
for a servant, till it was fairly over. She never
introduced, or connived at, miscellaneous conversation during its process. As she emphatically observed, cards were cards: and if ever I
saw unmingled distaste in her fine last-century
countenance, it was at the airs of a young gentleman of a literary turn, who had been with
difficulty persuaded to take a hand; and who, in
his excess of candour, declared, that he thought
there was no harm in unbending the mind now
and then, after serious studies, in recreations
of that kind! She could not bear to have
her noble occupation, to which she wound up her
faculties, considered in that light. It was her
business, her duty, the thing she came into the
world to do,—and she did it. She unbent
her mind afterwards—over a book. Pope was her
favourite author: his Rape of the Lock her
favourite work. She once did me the favour to
play over with me (with the cards) his celebrated
game of Ombre in that poem; and to explain to
me how far it agreed with, and in what points it
would be found to differ from, tradrille. Her
illustrations were apposite and poignant; and I
had the pleasure of sending the substance of
them to Mr. Bowles: but I suppose they came
too late to be inserted among his ingenious notes
upon that author."

(*b*) Write a descriptive paragraph about a

fruiterer's shop, using the following notes as a guide if necessary :—

The gaiety and colour of the window—the various fruit—where it comes from—the English fruit.

LESSON XIII

PUNCTUATION

Certain marks have been agreed upon by writers and printers so as to help readers to understand exactly what is meant by the written or printed page. The importance of these marks may be well shown in the two different meanings that may be attached to the following couplet found above a barber's door :—

What do you think
I'll shave you for nothing and give you a drink

There were no points at all, but the passer-by naturally took the view that here was an unusually generous offer. He read *What do you think ?* as an exclamation calling attention to the promise that follows. After the shave the barber punctuated it for himself—*What ! do you think I'll shave you for nothing and give you a drink ?*

The meaning of this sentence depends entirely upon its punctuation. This is regarded as a bad quality. The best sentence is that which stands least in need of punctuation. It is impossible to do without it altogether, but the aim of the good writer is to depend upon it as little as possible. Some books give very elaborate rules for the use of each of the punctuation marks, but these rules have the evil effect of giving them an undue importance in the mind of the writer. They must be servants, not masters.

The **full stop** or **period** need give no trouble, since it is only used to mark the end of a complete sentence that is neither a question nor an exclamation. Its use to indicate a contraction hardly enters into composition, though it is highly desirable that you should know the exact meaning of certain contractions—if only to avoid them in ordinary prose.

I.e. means that is (*id est*); *e.g.* means for example (*exempli gratiâ*); *viz.* means namely (*videlicet*); *&c.* or *etc.* means and so forth (*etcetera*).

These contractions are excellent things to omit, unless you happen to be an auctioneer or a catalogue-maker. In general, one should always take the trouble to write out *for example* if one wishes to use these words. In writing lists or purely explanatory matter where no pretence of style is made, all manner of intelligible contractions may be used. But in continuous prose it is an excellent rule to write out everything in full, even numbers.

The **comma** is unfortunate enough to labour under a great number of rules. Its duty is to show the slightest amount of separation that demands punctuation at all. It should be omitted wherever possible.

1. Simple sentences joined but not opposed to each other are separated by a comma. *A faint wind moaned through the trees, and Tom*

feared it might be the spirits of the dead complaining at being disturbed. " It's awful solemn like, ain't it ? "

2. Generally speaking, a series of words or phrases has its parts separated by commas :—

Conjuration, sleight of hand, magic, witch-craft, were the subjects of the evening.

The enemy waver, break, flee.

The brave, honest, dull Lefèvre died fighting against the captain he thought he was saving.

3. When the subject of a sentence is itself a clause or a longish phrase a comma is frequently placed after the subject :—

That the accused had been under the influence of drink when the man was killed, did not appear to the judge as an extenuating circumstance.

Speechless, abject reverence, with a blue coat and brass buttons, fails to express the porter's state of mind towards the six-hundred-pounders of the first landing.

4. An adjectival clause is marked off by commas when the qualifying clause does not indicate something essential in the thing qualified. *Du Maurier's house, which I saw lately, is now turned into some sort of Home.* But in the sentence, *How we like men who can be amused where most people would get into a passion,* we have no commas; for all that comes after *men* is really a part of the essential idea. We do not say that we like men in general, but only men-who-can-be-amused and the rest.

This rule may be shortly expressed : the copulative relative clause is marked off by commas, but not the restrictive (see Lesson IX).

Here the essentially parenthetical nature of clauses marked off by commas becomes evident. This is equally conspicuous in the next rule.

5. After an introductory phrase or word, before and after a term of address, and, indeed, generally before and after anything that may be omitted without altering the main sense of the sentence we may use the comma. Thus we have :—

Moreover, it does not pay.

Fetch me *Rasselas*, my dear, out of the book room.

The goddess Nicotine has a fund of good sense, which prompts her, as a general thing, to put a smile, either broad or latent, into the carving of her pipes and cigar-holders.

Here " *as a general thing* " and " *either broad or latent* " are both parenthetical. It must be admitted that the sentence, though by a good author, is over-punctuated. There are too many commas, which gives a jerkiness to the whole. The comma after *smile* and *latent* could go.

A real **parenthesis,** that is, one which is more markedly independent of its surroundings, is usually indicated by being enclosed within brackets ( ). Thus :—

He believed in her so much (often to his annoyance) that she was a religion to him.

The parenthesis should be used sparingly. It is a confession that something is being brought into the sentence that has no right to be there. It is less abused in the form of brackets than in that of the dash, which is becoming so common

78

as to threaten to take the place of all the other punctuation.

The **dash** (—) may be legitimately used to indicate a parenthesis, but it should be confined to those cases in which there is a more sudden break from the general run of the passage :—

In the unknown land called Markland, which may or may not have been Rhode Island, the Skrælings—and the Lord He knows who these may or may not have been—came to trade with the Vikings.

Another use of the dash is to indicate a conclusion without expressing it. This conclusion is quite clear to the hearer, though the speaker is unwilling to state it baldly :—

Business is business, and you may be sure I shouldn't give that price unless——

This use of the dash always implies a pause, though Scott thought it necessary to state this in the following passage :—

" ' I would rather work these ten bones to the knuckles, and live by my labour; but '—(and here he paused)."

A very common use of the dash is to indicate that what follows it is of special significance, or is not the natural or expected outcome of what goes before :—

Removing envelope after envelope with ever-increasing eagerness he finally disclosed—his own letter.

The **semicolon** (;) marks a slighter connection

between the parts of a sentence than does the comma : it is particularly useful in indicating contrasts :—

Permission was readily granted; and he set out for Italy.

The zeal of Burke was still fiercer; but it was far purer.

A very common use of the semicolon is to mark off parts of a long sentence that might quite naturally be separated by commas were it not that commas are already used largely in the sentence for subordinate divisions :—

Twice, while residing in the Writers' Buildings, he attempted to destroy himself; and twice the pistol which he snapped at his own head failed to go off.

Old-fashioned teachers of reading used to give their pupils the mechanical rule : at a comma stop as long as to count *one*, at a semicolon to count *two*, at a colon *three*, and at a full-stop *four*. This somewhat wooden plan was not very satisfactory in teaching reading, but it is at least useful in fixing in the pupils' minds the comparative degrees of separation indicated by the various marks.

The **colon** (:) does for a long sentence, containing semicolons and commas, what the semicolon does for one containing commas : it marks off broader distinctions than either of the other two. Thus :—

No person shall be permitted to visit more than one picture in one day : at which rate it would take at least three years to see a gallery of any extent; and true picture-lovers would probably confine their attentions to two or three favourites; spending day after day at their houses, not always gazing on the very canvas, but musing upon the fine symbolism of the surroundings, and leisurely accumulating fresh power to see and understand.

A very common use of the colon is to introduce the details of a group of things already referred to in the mass :—

The captain's excuses for not firing a royal salute were : first, he did not know that the king was on board; secondly, he was afraid lest the firing should cause a panic in the port; thirdly, his gunpowder had given out.

The **exclamation mark** (!) should be very sparingly used, particularly in prose. In no case should it be doubled (! !), however great the occasion.

The **question mark** (?) is to be used after every direct question, but never after an indirect.

Six men are to be hanged on the morrow : comes no hammering on the Rabenstein ? But in the indirect form,—*Carlyle asked why there came no hammering on the Rabenstein,*—there is no question mark.

The use of **quotation marks** (" ") is easily stated. They always enclose the very words that came out of the speaker's mouth, or are quoted direct from any author :—

" I can't get out," said the starling. But : The starling said that he could not get out.

Clearly the bird did not open its mouth and utter the words—*that he could not get out.* Accordingly these are not enclosed in quotation marks.

When a quotation occurs within a quotation the inner quotation is marked by single points

(' '), as in this passage from Meredith : " Beauchamp continued in the street : ' Tyrannies like this fellow's have made the English the dullest and wretchedest people in Europe ' ".

Capital letters are necessary at the beginning of every sentence, at the first word of every line of verse, at the beginning of every direct quotation. All proper nouns are written with capitals, the pronoun I, the vocative O, and all names applied to the Deity. In the titles of books or chapters all the important words have capitals— only articles, demonstratives, prepositions and little adverbs beginning with small letters. The days of the week, the months of the year, the great festivals, and generally any outstanding thing or event—the House of Commons, the Reformation—are dignified with capitals. Note particularly that adjectives formed from proper nouns retain the capital—Chinese, Lenten. A personified word (see Lesson XIV) is written with a capital.

Exercise 13

Punctuate the following, insert capitals where necessary, and arrange any verse into its proper lines :—

(*a*) 1. A man going to sea his wife desires the prayers of the congregation. 2. The woman that deliberates is lost. 3. Ask wheres the north at york tis on the tweed in scotland at the orcades and there at greenland zembla or the lord knows where. 4. At length mary died elizabeth succeeded and cecil rose at once to greatness. 5. And what did your uncle say to that asked the judge he said you must never breathe a word of this to a living soul was the reply.   6. I go to a convention of philanthropists do what I can I cannot keep my eyes off the clock but if there should appear in the company some gentle soul who knows little of persons or parties of carolina or cuba but who announces a law that disposes these particulars and so certifies me of the equity which checkmates every false player bankrupts every self seeker and apprises me of my independence on any conditions of country or time or human body that man liberates me I forget the clock I pass out of the sore relation to persons I am healed of my hurts I am made immortal by apprehending my possession of incorruptible goods.   7. If he was an inhumane old gentleman and I am afraid it is a fact that he was inhumane he was also perfectly intrepid.   8. He promised to go down first and boldly he did so for william give him his due had the heart of a lion.   9. Im no leech said adam let me go no not yet I will convict thee of ignorance thou dost not even know where the liver is placed I do answered adam shortly but what then thou dost I deny it here is a pin stick it into this wax man where thou sayest the liver lies in the human frame adam unsuspiciously obeyed.   10. You and I master worthy have worked hard many years and think it very well to have scraped a trifle of money together you a few hundreds I suppose and I a few thousands.

(*b*) Punctuate the following conversation between Alice in Wonderland, the Hatter and the March Hare, insert capitals and apostrophes, and break it up into paragraphs :—

there was a table set out under a tree in front of the house and the march hare and the hatter were having tea at it a dormouse was sitting between them fast asleep and the other two were using it as a cushion resting their elbows on it and talking over its head very uncomfortable for the dormouse thought alice only as its asleep i suppose it doesnt mind the table was a large one but the three were all crowded together at one corner of it no room no room they cried out when they saw alice coming theres plenty of room said alice indignantly and she sat down in a large armchair at one end of the table have some wine the march hare said in an encouraging tone alice looked all round the table but there was nothing on it but tea i dont see any wine she remarked there isn't any said the march hare then it wasn't very civil of you to offer it said alice angrily it wasn't very civil of you to sit down without being invited said the march hare i didn't know it was your table said alice its laid for a great many more than three your hair wants cutting said the hatter he had been looking at alice for some time with great curiosity and this was his first speech you should learn not to make personal remarks alice said with some severity its very rude the hatter opened his eyes very wide on hearing this but all he said was why is a raven like a writing desk come we shall have some fun now thought alice im glad theyve begun asking riddles i believe i can guess that she added aloud do you mean that you think you can find out the answer to it said the march hare exactly so said alice then you should say what you mean the march hare went on i do alice hastily replied at least at least i mean what i say thats the same thing you know

LESSON XIV

ORNAMENT—FIGURATIVE SPEECH

We have been considering so far the structure of prose, and we have now to consider its external graces, which, for want of a better name, we may call ornament. The writer, like the architect and the designer, has now a problem to face. What part shall ornament play in the whole? How far can use and elegance be combined? How he answers these questions will depend on his own taste and the taste of his age. To writers in the sixteenth and seventeenth centuries, ornament seemed all-important. They did not study composition, but rhetoric—which is the art of ornament: their books of rhetoric were categories of the various figures of speech. Taste has changed, and most modern writers prefer a simpler style. This is certainly better for the student, and he will do well to imitate a plain prose style. He may admire the richly decorated style of G. K. Chesterton, but it is not one to be imitated—if indeed imitation were possible. The writer, like the designer, must use ornament sparingly if he is to use it with effect. He must take care also to use it in the right place and for the right subject, or it will appear as ridiculous as a fine lady tripping down a country lane in gold-brocaded shoes.

Ornament commonly takes the form of figurative speech. We are not satisfied with a plain term, and choose a more imaginative way to express our meaning. We say—*His reproaches cut her to the quick*, which is of course literally impossible, but is more emphatic than saying simply—" His reproaches hurt her ". Here a comparison is implied between the mental pain she feels at his reproaches, and the physical pain she would feel if she were stabbed with a knife. Such implied comparisons are called *metaphors*. When a comparison is actually made, we call it a *simile*. In the sentence, *The ungodly flourish like a green bay tree* we use a simile; but if we say, *The ungodly flourish and bear goodly fruit*, then we use a metaphor. Similes are often worked out at some length, and include several points of comparison, while a metaphor is often expressed in a single word.

Our language is full of metaphors. We frequently use them quite unconsciously. When we talk about the *bed* of a river, the *shoulder* of a mountain, the *hands* of a watch, the *key* of a position, we are apt to think that we are using literal language, and so, for practical purposes, we are. A considerable proportion of our vocabulary was originally metaphorical, but by long use the comparison has become so unobtrusive that we do not observe it unless our attention is specially called to it. Such dead metaphors do not serve to quicken the imagination. If you wish to make a vivid comparison, then you must make up a metaphor or simile for yourself.

Milton is content to say *When the dappled dawn doth rise*. This is literal. Homer is fond of talking of *Rosy-fingered Morn.* Here we have a kind of metaphor. Kipling gives us : *And the dawn comes up like thunder*, which is a simile. In the Homeric metaphor we have the dawn compared to a person, and this kind of metaphor usually gets the name of **personification.** When we make the sea greedy or justice lame or love tyrannical we are using personification just as much as when we let the trees clap their hands. It is customary to write the personified word with a capital.

When we turn aside from our main subject to address some person or thing that is not present, we use the figure called **apostrophe,** as in the familiar " O woman, in our hours of ease," etc.

Some other forms of figurative speech resemble metaphor. If two things are so closely associated that the mention of one recalls the other, then the most vivid word is sometimes used, as in this sentence, *The armoured train vomited khaki.* Here the verb implies a metaphor, but the word khaki stands for soldiers, not from any likeness between the stuff and the men, but because the two are firmly connected in our minds. In the same way, *The Crescent fell before the Cross* means that the followers of Mahomet were defeated by the Christians. Again, a part may stand for the whole in such a sentence as, *All the blue bonnets are over the Border*, or *Eighteen lances could hold that pass against an army*. Sometimes an individual is made to stand for a class, or the abstract for the concrete, as thus :—

Her salon attracted the learning of a dozen provinces.

Mr. Lloyd George is the Peter Pan of politics.
or, to take a more modern example :—

The deliberations of the parish council seem to be directly guided by Colonel Blimp.

A comparison sustained through a long passage, and worked into a story, becomes an *allegory*. We are given a plain story with a clear surface meaning, and a less apparent under-meaning. The parables of the New Testament are little allegories, told by way of illustrating general truths. In our own literature, *The Pilgrim's Progress* and *Gulliver's Travels* are well-known allegories, which are read and enjoyed by children for the sake of the story, yet have a profound underlying seriousness. Interesting modern examples of allegory are *The Happy Hypocrite* by Max Beerbohm, and Rebecca West's novel, *Harriet Hume*.

Many writers have a natural tendency towards figurative speech, but such a tendency must be held in check. Over-use of metaphor and simile destroys their value, and often produces the absurdities of mixed metaphor. This most often occurs when one writes or speaks in " the grand manner " :—

Let us build our house upon a sure foundation, that its life-blood be not sapped, and the waves of enmity and malice wash not over us.

Here the metaphors from house-building, trees, blood and stormy seas are wildly mixed. It is not enough to apologise for a mixed metaphor by such a phrase as, " if we may change the metaphor ". If you feel the necessity for apology, then it is time you considered how your sentence may be amended. In general, use metaphor sparingly, unless you have especial need to make some detail emphatic, or have to express an abstract meaning in concrete form, or are describing something that cannot easily be expressed in plain terms. Milton, when he describes Hell in *Paradise Lost*, cannot make it real to his readers except by constant comparison and simile, since no one can imagine what Hell is like except by comparing it to the familiar things of earth. If you wish to describe a fire, or a great storm, or a wild sea, or anything else which is not part of normal everyday experience, then you will naturally fall back on comparisons to make your meaning clear. Stevenson uses metaphor and simile sparingly and always with justification, as in this description of a storm in the Hebrides :—

" All round the isle of Aros the surf, with an incessant, hammering thunder, beat upon the reefs and beaches. Now louder in one place, now lower in another, like the combinations of orchestral music, the constant mass of sound was hardly varied for a moment. And loud above all this hurly-burly I could hear the changeful voices of the Roost, and the intermittent roaring of the Merry Men. The noise of them seemed almost mirthful, as it out-topped the other noises of the night ; or if not mirthful, yet instinct with a portentous joviality. Nay, and it seemed even human. As when savage men have drunk away their reason, and discarding speech, bawl together in their madness by the hour ; so, to my ears, these deadly breakers shouted by Aros in the night."

Exercise 14

(*a*) Write out the meaning of each sentence in plain literal language, and say which forms you think most suitable.

1. Babies rolled about like tumbled fruit in grass. 2. Shut your 'ead. 3. Lovers' watches stand still. 4. The ashes of Mr. Foster's note seemed to crinkle into a sour grin. 5. Literature had jilted him; henceforth Law was to be his mistress. 6. That shop, which was dark and smelt of Bibles, was a loadstone rock for all that bore the name of boy. 7. Habit is habit, and not to be flung out of the window by any man, but coaxed downstairs a step at a time. 8. Do you hear the wood crying for us? It's sorry for our little troubles. 9. There are always plenty of men ready to lick the blacking off one's boots provided always that that doubtful fare be varied by champagne and truffles at appropriate intervals. 10. Mrs. Agar toyed with a biscuit. 11. The lid of the kettle clattered like a deaf and dumb young cymbal that had never known the use of its twin-brother. 12. An Ogilvie's sword never ploughed so deep a furrow. 13. His evil soul went down to its place squeaking, like a bat into the darkness of a cave. 14. "No," said his daughter, taking a weapon of fine cambric out of her pocket. 15. With these words he retired, leaving a seething volcano to pace the deck.

(*b*) Find a metaphor and a simile for each of the following :—a rocket, a sailing ship, flood water.

LESSON XV

SOME OTHER FORMS OF ORNAMENT

Several recognised ornaments of style owe their effect to the force of contrast. In what is called antitheses the contrast is expressly stated.

Coleridge tells us that his teacher flogged him on a certain occasion, " wisely, I think, soundly, I know ". Here we have a double contrast plainly stated—*wisely, soundly*; *think, know*. Sometimes the contrast gains point by one part being left out. In that most familiar figure known as **irony** the contrast is between the surface statement which is pleasant, and the underlying truth which is bitter. It is ironical to dismiss a candidate for an assistant-clerkship in the Foreign Office with the words, " I'm very sorry we have no vacancy worthy of your talents. You see, the Prime Minister *will* not retire." In the still more popular figure of **hyperbole** the contrast is between the plain truth and the deliberately exaggerated statement of it. When we say that the trees of California are very tall, we use the words of truth and soberness; when we declare that they are so high that it takes two men and a boy to look at the top of them, we drop into hyperbole.

To the class of figures of contrast belong those witty sayings called **epigrams.** An epigram must be short, pointed, with enough falsehood to make it piquant and with enough truth to make it worth saying :—*A science is nothing but a well-made language. A man who has stolen sixty thousand pounds ought to be able to live* *honestly.* Another contrast figure, known as **euphemism,** consists in putting things in an unduly favourable way. It may be kindly meant, as when we call a shoemaker a leather merchant, or it may only intensify the disagreeable fact it seems to palliate, as in *the independent candidate nowhere showed his independence so markedly as in relation to the truth.*

Another class of figures of speech depend largely upon the order in which ideas are expressed. If we arrange ideas in the order of increasing intensity or importance we have what is known as **climax.** *Swiftly Napoleon mounted— lieutenant, general, First Consul, Emperor.* It is not always easy to have a climax so accurately graded as this. Often some of the terms will be understood in a different way by various readers. In the following example from Sir Walter Scott's *Woodstock* we have a double climax in which Sir Henry Lee relieves his mind about two of his political opponents. " What ! John Milton, the blasphemous and bloody-minded author of the *Defensio Populi Anglicani* ! —the advocate of the infernal High Court of Fiends !—the creature and parasite of that grand impostor, that loathsome hypocrite, that detestable monster, that prodigy of the universe, that disgrace of mankind, that landscape of iniquity, that sink of sin, and that compendium of baseness, Oliver Cromwell ! " Here the old cavalier is so eager to vent his anger that he does not take time to arrange his abuse in exact order of merit. But while we may quarrel about which of the old gentleman's epithets is the most stinging, we cannot but agree that the effect of the whole goes on increasing, and that, therefore, the figure is a genuine climax.

When the climax breaks down, whether by accident or by the deliberate design of the writer, we have anti-climax. *Our hills and dales, our hearths and homes, our wives and daughters, our flocks and herds, lie at the mercy of the invaders.* Here everything goes well till the end. The *flocks and herds* should come in after the *hills and dales.* Note that anti-climax does not mean a descending order, but a sudden drop from a height. " A month to consider it ! Not a week, not a day, an hour, a minute ! I demand instant submission." Here we have really an ascending order of imperious demand, though the time periods are in descending order.

Inversion is a figure that is very commonly used to give emphasis and variety. It consists in reversing the usual order of words, particularly of subject and predicate. It is very common in verse, so common as to be almost the normal construction there. *As bends the bark's mast in the gale.* In prose it may be very effectively used as in, *Pitiful is the case of the blind who cannot read the face ; pitiful that of the deaf who cannot follow the changes of the voice.* But this figure seems peculiarly liable to abuse by those who seek to be effective in common speech. It is barbarous to write *Understood him she has not.*

Alliteration is more often used in poetry than in prose. It consists in using words beginning with the same letter or sound, and when used with restraint it can be very effective,—as in *Macbeth*,

" Duncan is in his grave,
After life's fitful fever he sleeps well."

In prose it is often used in hack phrases, which

should be earnestly avoided; *fair, fat and forty*; *happy Hampstead*; *ministerial mendacity*. Yet it can be used in prose with exquisite effect, as in this passage from Kingsley's *Water Babies*, where the same sounds are not too often repeated :—

" And what sort of river was it? Was it like an Irish stream, winding through the brown bogs, where the wild ducks squatter up from among the white water-lilies, and the curlews flit to and fro, crying ' Tullie-wheep, mind your sheep '; and Dennis tells you strange stories of the Peishtamore, the great bogy-snake which lies in the black peat pools, among the old pine-stems, and puts his head out at night to snap at the cattle as they come down to drink? "

Exercise 15

State which figure of speech each of the following exemplifies, and write out the meaning of each sentence in plain literal language :—

1. As a dog doesn't comprehend good English we naturally talk bad to him. 2. Let us endeavour so to live that when we come to die even the undertaker will be sorry. 3. The Duke of Wellington's English despatches were written in fine idiomatic English—and so were his French ones. 4. Some German words are so long that they have a perspective. 5. Women hate a debt as men a gift. 6. In order to love mankind we must expect little from them. 7. The bareness of the hills in the south of Scotland is such that a bluebottle can be seen against the sky when it walks along their pro-file. 8. We are near awakening when we dream

that we were dreaming. 9. The love-light was in her eyes, but Andrew did not open the door for her, for he was a Scotch graduate. Besides, she might one day be his wife. 10. Paris is not a city, but a Bedlam. 11. It is better to be a young June-bug than an old bird of paradise. 12. And the verse halts like the best of Luther's psalms. 13. If we still love those we lose can we altogether lose those we love? 14. Absence destroys small passions and increases great ones, as the wind extinguishes tapers and kindles fires. 15. The prime minister was set free from the cares of office.

LESSON XVI

DIRECT AND REPORTED SPEECH

When we give the very words used by a speaker we are said to use the direct form. " I can't get out," cried the starling, is an example of this direct form. The starling opened his mouth and out came these actual words : " I can't get out ". In reported speech this would have to read something like this : *The starling said that it* (or *he*, if you prefer that form) *could not get out.* Thus the tense is always changed to the past in reported speech, and the person of verbs and pronouns is changed.

There are other changes too. " Here stand I," said Luther, is the direct form, and becomes *Luther said that he stood there.* Thus *here* is changed to *there.* Similarly *this* becomes *that.*

The best way to get a real knowledge of the

difference between the two forms is to practise turning passages from the one to the other.

It is more difficult turning from the direct to the indirect, for there are often a great number of *he's* and *him's* that are apt to get confounded. This confusion is usually avoided by inserting a proper name in brackets after the doubtful pronoun.

Ellicock said to Wilberforce that his father had bought him the gold watch that he was then wearing. Here we are not sure whose father bought the watch, for whom the watch was bought, who was then wearing it. The probable meaning is, *Ellicock said to Wilberforce that his* (Ellicock's) *father had bought him* (Ellicock) *the gold watch that he* (Ellicock) *was then wearing.* This labelling of pronouns is better than confusion—*anything* is better than lack of clearness. But the expedient is very clumsy and should be avoided. It may be pardoned in a reported speech; but in a piece of original composition it is a public confession of faulty construction.

" There is nothing at all unusual in this, and I have no doubt Burke would have stuck to his bargain, had not Hamilton conceived the fatal idea that Burke's brains were *exclusively* his (Hamilton's)."

Here the clumsiness could be averted, and the author's point equally well made, by saying, ". . . had not Hamilton conceived the fatal idea that he had bought the *exclusive* use of Burke's brains ".

In the following exercises, in turning from the direct to the reported form you will find it necessary to make occasional use of the noun in parenthesis. You must try to avoid the construction so far as is possible by repeating the noun in the text as often as that can be done without unseemly repetition.

Exercise 16

Change the passages (*a*) and (*b*) into the direct form, and passages (*c*) and (*d*) into the reported form.

(*a*) Mr. Wetherell said that he had half guessed there might be some hanky-panky of this sort, and he had therefore taken such steps as would prevent him from being left out in the cold. He proposed to deal with this affair as he dealt with matters of politics or of organisation, in that he should use plain language, and speak out his mind like a man. If a man or a woman behaved straight to him, he behaved straight to them; if *they* behaved crooked, *he* behaved crooked. That was him all the world over. Mr. Wetherell added that if he were then and there to undertake to write his own epitaph, he would simply take a pen, dip it in the ink, seat himself at the table, and write these words : " He was as open as the day ".

(*b*) Mr. PICKWICK observed (says the secretary) that fame was dear to the heart of every man. Poetic fame was dear to the heart of his friend Snodgrass; the fame of conquest was equally dear to his friend Tupman; and the desire of earning fame in the sports of the field, the air, and the water, was uppermost in the breast of his friend Winkle. He (Mr. Pickwick) would not deny that he was influenced by human passions, and human feelings—(cheers)—possibly

by human weaknesses—(loud cries of " No ");
but this he would say, that if ever the fire of
self-importance broke out in his bosom, the
desire to benefit the human race in preference
effectually quenched it. The praise of mankind
was his Swing; philanthropy was his insurance
office. (Vehement cheering.) He had felt some
pride—he acknowledged it freely, and let his
enemies make the most of it—he had felt some
pride when he presented his Tittlebatian Theory
to the world; it might be celebrated or it might
not. (A cry of " It is ", and great cheering.)
He would take the assertion of that honourable
Pickwickian whose voice he had just heard—it
was celebrated; but if the fame of that treatise
were to extend to the farthest confines of the
known world, the pride with which he should
reflect on the authorship of that production
would be as nothing compared with the pride
with which he looked around him on this, the
proudest moment of his existence. (Cheers.)
He was a humble individual. (" No, no.")
Still he could not but feel that they had selected
him for a service of great honour, and of some
danger. Travelling was in a troubled state, and
the minds of coachmen were unsettled. Let
them look abroad and contemplate the scenes
which are enacting around them. Stage coaches
were upsetting in all directions, horses were
bolting, boats were overturning, and boilers were
bursting. (Cheers—a voice, " No ".) No !
(Cheers.) Let that honourable Pickwickian who
cried " No " so loudly come forward and deny
it, if he could. (Cheers.) Who was it that
cried " No "? (Enthusiastic cheering.) Was it
some vain and disappointed man—he would not

say haberdasher—(loud cheers)—who, jealous of
the praise which had been—perhaps undeservedly
—bestowed on his (Mr. Pickwick's) researches,
and smarting under the censure which had been
heaped upon his own feeble attempts at rivalry,
now took this vile and calumnious mode of—

Mr. BLOTTON (of Aldgate) rose to order. Did
the honourable Pickwickian allude to him?
(Cries of "Order", "Chair", "Yes", "No",
" Go on ", " Leave off ", etc.)

Mr. PICKWICK would not put up to be put
down by clamour. He *had* alluded to the
honourable gentleman. (Great excitement.)

Mr. BLOTTON would only say then, that he
repelled the hon. gent.'s false and scurrilous
accusation with profound contempt. (Great
cheering.) The hon. gent. was a humbug.

(*c*) Sir,—The atrocious crime of being a young
man, which the honourable gentleman has, with
such spirit and decency, charged upon me, I
shall neither attempt to palliate nor deny; but
content myself with wishing, that I may be one
of those whose follies may cease with their
youth, and not of those who continue ignorant
in spite of age and experience.

Whether youth can be attributed to any man
as a reproach, I will not, Sir, assume the province
of determining; but surely, age may justly
become contemptible, if the opportunities which
it brings have passed away without improvement, and vice appear to prevail when the
passions have subsided. The wretch who, after
having seen the consequences of a thousand
errors, continues still to blunder, and in whom
age has only added obstinacy to stupidity, is
surely the object either of abhorrence or con-

tempt; and deserves not that his grey head should secure him from insults. Much more, Sir, is he to be abhorred, who, as he has advanced in age, has receded from virtue, and become more wicked with less temptation; who prostitutes himself for money which he cannot enjoy, and spends the remains of his life in the ruin of his country.

(*d*) I cannot, my Lords, I will not, join in congratulation on misfortune and disgrace. This, my Lords, is a perilous and tremendous moment. It is not a time for adulation; the smoothness of flattery cannot save us in this rugged and awful crisis. It is now necessary to instruct the throne in the language of truth. We must, if possible, dispel the delusion and darkness which envelop it; and display, in its full danger and genuine colours, the ruin which is brought to our doors. Can ministers still presume to expect support in their infatuation? Can Parliament be so dead to its dignity and duty, as to give its support to measures thus obtruded and forced upon it? Measures, my Lords, which have reduced this late flourishing empire to scorn and contempt! " But yesterday, and Britain might have stood against the world : now, none so poor as do her reverence ! " —The people, whom we at first despised as rebels, but whom we now acknowledge as enemies, are abetted against us, supplied with every military store, have their interests consulted, and their ambassadors entertained, by our inveterate enemy; and ministers do not— and dare not—interpose with dignity or effect. The desperate state of our army abroad is in part known. No man more highly esteems and

honours the British troops than I do; I know
their virtues and their valour; I know they
can achieve anything but impossibilities; and
I know that the conquest of British America is
an impossibility. You cannot, my Lords, you
can not conquer America. What is your present
situation there? We do not know the worst;
but we know that in three campaigns we have
done nothing, and suffered much. You may
swell every expense, accumulate every assistance, and extend your traffic to the shambles
of every German despot : your attempts will
be for ever vain and impotent.

LESSON XVII

WRITING IN THIRD PERSON

There is a formal kind of composition that
sometimes takes the place of a letter. It is
marked by the exclusive use of the third person
where one would naturally expect the first and
the second. It is the recognised language of
invitations, particularly when these are of a
public or formal character. " The Mayor and
Corporation of Blanktown request the pleasure
of Mr. Dash's presence at dinner in the Town
Hall, on Thursday, the 24th March, 1938, at
7.30 P.M." The regulation reply is : " Mr. Dash
has much pleasure in accepting the invitation
of the Mayor and Corporation of Blanktown to
dinner in the Town Hall, on Thursday, the 24th
March, 1938, at 7.30 P.M."

Those who claim to be authorities on these

D

matters maintain that the reply should repeat all the details, as in Mr. Dash's specimen, and perhaps it is as well to gratify form-lovers by giving them plenty of form. The argument in favour of this fullness is that all chance of misunderstanding is thus removed. Invitations in the third person are used in private life wherever a certain formality is kept up. An invitation in the third person from an intimate friend ought to imply a specially good dinner.

A very common error in replying to invitations is to use the future instead of the present. "Mr. Dash-Blank will have much pleasure in accepting the kind invitation of . . ." This should read "has much pleasure". Mr. Dash-Blank does not intend to accept the invitation, he is accepting it as he writes. The confusion is caused by thinking of the dinner rather than of the invitation.

Another and less pleasant use of the third person is in communicating with people with whom we wish to have nothing to do, beyond the business of the moment. A lady writes to learn from another, who is not of her circle, the character of a servant. This is the sort of reply that comes. "Mrs. Dash-Blank has always found Susan Liskens careful, honest, and willing. She has been in her service only nine months, but she came to her with a four years' character, and has done nothing to forfeit it. She leaves her of her own accord."

The *she's* and *her's* are a little mixed, but no serious misunderstanding can arise. The following presents more difficulty :—

"Mr. Brown presents his compliments to

Mr. Johnson, and will be much obliged if he will keep his dog on his own side of the wall during the day, and on the other side of the house during the night, as neither he nor Mrs. Brown get a wink of sleep while he occupies his present position."

Bad as this is, it does not fall into the worst error of all—that of mixing up different persons. The writer gets tired of the formal third person, and drops into a more natural form.

" If advertiser RS 4309 will call at 47 Arlington Villas he will find a suite of rooms that fulfil all the conditions he specifies. Mrs. Spross can assure him that nothing will be wanting on her part to make him comfortable. I do my own washing so you can rely upon your linen being well attended to."

The whole style of writing is cumbersome and stilted. It is to be avoided as far as possible, but when it has to be used there must be no lapses into first or second person. Ambiguity may to a great extent be avoided by the frequent repetition of the proper names. This is perhaps not very elegant, but the style is already so clumsy that nothing can make it much worse.

Exercise 17

Rewrite the three examples of third personal composition in the preceding lesson, improving them wherever you see a chance.

LESSON XVIII

OBSCURITY AND AMBIGUITY

A sentence or a passage is obscure when it is difficult to gather the meaning. It may be that there *is* no meaning, as in the irritating conundrum, *Why is a mouse when it spins?* and its aggravating answer, *Because the fewer the higher*. In this case the lack of meaning is concealed only for a moment, but sometimes a long passage of apparently reasonable words conveys no real meaning to the mind. The following is quoted by an eminent psychologist, who confesses that he fails to make any sort of sense out of it.

" The flow of the efferent fluids of all these vessels from their outlets at the terminal loop of each culminate link on the surface of the nuclear organism is continuous as their respective atmospheric fruitage up to the altitudinal limit of their expansibility, whence, when atmosphered by like but coalescing essences from higher altitudes—those sensibly expressed as the essential qualities of external forms—they descend, and become assimilated by the afferents of the nuclear organism."

These are extreme cases. A writer usually has a meaning behind his words.

" We mean only a man having some sort of arms—a club, or a dart, or a matchlock, or a poker—anything which would give him the idea that he had to fight, and which would perhaps delay his death a moment while myriads of others swept over those who had killed him."

The man who wrote this meant to say that

an undisciplined and ill-armed horde, if only numerous enough, could overcome the best drilled and equipped army by the mere process of keeping the soldiers so busy killing some of the rabble that the rest of the rabble would have time to swarm over the soldiers and overcome them by sheer avoirdupois weight.

To convey this meaning the whole sentence after the words " his death a moment " would require to be re-cast, and might run thus, . . . " while myriads of his comrades swarmed over those who were in the act of killing him ". In this case the sentence has had to be expanded ; for the obscurity arises from the brevity of the explanation.

Speaking generally, it may be said that writers who are thoroughly at home in their subject are liable to become obscure because they take too much for granted. They themselves see so clearly the connection between cause and effect that they think it unnecessary to state many things which are plain to them, but are quite unknown to ordinary readers. Learned men who seek to popularise their subjects almost always become obscure by omitting certain steps in their reasoning.

In Lord Bacon's essays we find excellent examples of the advantages and defects of a condensed style. No words are wasted, and wherever the sense does not suffer there is a clear gain. But very frequently Bacon's economy of words leads to unnecessary labour on the part of his readers. In the very first essay we find this sentence : " Doth any man doubt, that if there were taken out of men's minds, vain opinions, flattering hopes, false valuations, imaginations as one would, and the like; but it would leave the minds of a number of men, poor shrunken things ". The phrase *imaginations as one would* is an unduly condensed way of saying the habit of trying to persuade ourselves that things are what our desires would have them to be. Sometimes this condensation is justifiable, since it takes the form of an epigram in which the charm lies in getting at the true meaning through an apparently inadequate expression. " It is good that a man's face give his tongue leave to speak ", is a more striking way of conveying the meaning—*A man should not betray his thoughts by the expression of his face, but should make disclosures only by his tongue.* In the following examples, however, the gain in force is more than counter-balanced by the loss in clearness :—

The master of superstition is the people.	The real origin of superstition is not with the people, but there is in them a predisposition to be deceived.
And they would be thought wits of direction.	They desire to be considered able men who are capable of directing others.
Finally he waxeth wiser than himself.	He becomes wiser than he could become without the advice of some friend.
But ignorance severally disguised.	But ignorance concealing itself under various forms.
A wound or solution of continuity.	A severance of parts of the body that ought to be joined.

| Alchemy pretendeth to make separation of all the unlike parts of bodies, which in mixtures of nature are incorporate. | . . . which are incorporated in substances as these substances are found in nature. |

It is easy to understand how a passage may become obscure through lack of sufficient words. At first sight it may seem impossible to become obscure by using too many words. It would appear that the only evil result would be a weariness rising from the repetition of explanations of matters already clearly understood. But in two ways excess of words darkens knowledge. In the first way the meaning is lost in its expression : there is such a small idea hidden away among such a heap of words that it becomes difficult to dig it out. In the second place every word that is used in composition is understood to mean something that is necessary to the sense of the passage in which it occurs. The orator who maintained that it was " cowardly to shoot bad landlords in Ireland " obscured his meaning, unless, indeed, he really meant that it was not cowardly to shoot good landlords so long as they did not happen to be in Ireland.

A very common form of obscurity in writing is known as ambiguity. When a sentence may convey either of two meanings it is said to be ambiguous. "The duke yet lives that Henry shall depose," is a case of deliberate ambiguity. If you think over the sentence for a moment, you will see that it does not tell which of the two—Henry or the duke—is to depose the other. So in ancient history we read of a king who was assured by an oracle that if he invaded a certain country he would " destroy a great kingdom ". When this king was defeated and complained of the falsehood of the oracle, he was reminded that the oracle had not stated whose great kingdom was to be destroyed. The king had jumped to the conclusion that the prophecy had only one meaning : the oracle knew it had two.

There is no snare more difficult to avoid than this same ambiguity. The preceding paragraph was meant to illustrate the vice, but not quite in the way it is illustrated in the concluding clause, " the oracle knew it had two ". Here *it* may mean either the prophecy or the oracle. It was meant to mean the prophecy, but since the oracle may be treated as neuter, there is no escape. The clause is ambiguous. This word *it* is, indeed, a particularly troublesome one. *She held the tea-cup to her cheek to keep it warm.* You might bring forward many arguments for believing that it was the cheek that was being kept warm, and as many in favour of the tea-cup. The relative pronoun sometimes causes ambiguity. *The castle was taken from him by William Rufus, son of the Conqueror, who had made the original grant.* Since the relative should always be allocated to the nearest legitimate antecedent, this sentence should mean that William, the son of the Conqueror, had taken away the castle, but that the original grant had been made by the Conqueror himself. If Rufus both made the grant and withdrew it, the sentence should run : *The castle was taken from him by the Conqueror's son, William Rufus, who had made the original grant.*

In the following exercise write out clearly each of the two possible meanings, after this fashion. 1. (a) The duke yet lives who shall depose Henry. 1. (b) The duke yet lives whom Henry shall depose. 2. (a) If you invade that country you will destroy the great nation which inhabits it. 2. (b) If you invade that country you will destroy your own great nation. 3. (a) To keep her cheek warm she held the tea-cup to it. 3. (b) To keep the tea-cup warm she held it to her cheek.

Exercise 18

In each case mark with the letter (a) the meaning that you think the writer intended to convey.

1. For do I now persuade God or men? 2. We know little individually of his hearers. 3. I shall lose no time in reading your verses. 4. Drink to me only with thine eyes. 5. From that place where fixed you be by His decree you cannot pass. 6. The only work we have seen in the exhibition by James Collinson is a small portrait of Christina G. Rossetti, sister of Rossetti, and a poor thing. 7. They forget that character makes the man and not the profession. 8. That is either a man or a woman's voice. 9. For sale a fine bull dog. Eats anything. Very fond of children. 10. The fearful creatures stealthily approached the edge of the precipice.

LESSON XIX

VERBOSITY, PLEONASM, TAUTOLOGY

Tautology and pleonasm are forms of the vice of using more words than are necessary to express our meaning. By many writers the two terms are treated as synonymous, but others try to establish a distinction. Tautology is said to mean the repetition of the same idea in different words, while pleonasm is the use of words of which the meaning is implied in words already employed. Thus it is tautological to say, *The earth under the trees was wet, damp and moist*, or, *You may enter this show free, gratis and for nothing*. Examples of pleonasm are, *I have seen it with my own eyes. The two friends went for a walking tour through France on foot.*

Still other writers are inclined to call all the above examples tautologies, and prefer to limit pleonasm to the vice of adding words which convey nothing really new, though their meaning is not actually implied in any previous expression. *This club treats all other clubs with an eye of contempt*. Here *an eye of* is obviously pleonastic.

Verbosity is the general name for the vice of wordiness. Tautology and pleonasm are forms of verbosity, but there are many other forms. Talkative persons and diffuse writers may never actually repeat their ideas, but they frequently use a very large number of words to express a very small number of ideas.

We shall now proceed to begin to illustrate this objectionable vice of verbosity by referring to a passage that may be found in the pages of a well-known author, or rather authoress, who, however, must not be held responsible for the high-sounding but somewhat empty and frivolous maunderings which she puts into the mouth of a rather austere and very precise old maiden lady who is delightfully portrayed in the charming chapters of that gem of Mrs. Gaskell's art—*Cranford.*

That paragraph is a verbose way of making the simple statement : Miss Jenkyns, in *Cranford*, is responsible for the following example of verbosity.

" The Honourable Mrs. Jamieson has only just quitted me; and, in the course of conversation, she communicated to me the intelligence that she had yesterday received a call from her revered husband's quondam friend, Lord Mauleverer. You will not easily conjecture what brought his lordship within the precincts of our little town. It was to see Captain Brown, with whom, it appears, his lordship was acquainted in the 'plumed wars', and who had the privilege of averting destruction from his lordship's head when some great peril was impending over it, off the misnomered Cape of Good Hope. You know our friend the Honourable Mrs. Jamieson's deficiency in the spirit of innocent curiosity; and you will therefore not be so much surprised when I tell you she was quite unable to disclose to me the exact nature of the peril in question. I was anxious, I confess, to ascertain in what manner Captain Brown, with his limited establishment, could receive so distinguished a guest; and I discovered that his lordship retired to rest,

and, let us hope, to refreshing slumbers, at the
Angel Hotel; but shared the Brunonian meals
during the two days that he honoured Cranford
with his august presence. Mrs. Johnston, our
civil butcher's wife, informs me that Miss Jessie
purchased a leg of lamb; but, besides this, I
can hear of no preparation whatever to give a
suitable reception to so distinguished a visitor.
Perhaps they entertained him with ' the feast
of reason and the flow of soul '; and to us,
who are acquainted with Captain Brown's sad
want of relish for ' the pure wells of English
undefiled ', it may be matter for congratulation
that he has had the opportunity of improving
his taste by holding converse with an elegant
and refined member of the British aristocracy.
But from some mundane failings who is altogether free ? "

Another form of verbosity arises from feeble-
ness of thought. A person who cannot select
the essential parts of his subject becomes verbose by introducing a wearisome series of unimportant details. One thing recalls another
and the speaker instead of directing his speech
is directed by it. This is well illustrated in the
following extract from Miss Austen's *Emma* :—

" ' But where could *you* hear it ? ' cried Miss
Bates. ' Where could you possibly hear it,
Mr. Knightley? For it is not five minutes
since I received Mrs. Cole's note—no, it cannot
be more than five—or at least ten—for I had
got my bonnet and spencer on, just ready to
come out—I was only gone down to speak to
Patty again about the pork—Jane was standing
in the passage—were not you, Jane?—for my
mother was so afraid that we had not any salt-

ing-pan large enough. So I said I would go down and see, and Jane said, " Shall I go down instead? for I think you have a little cold, and Patty has been washing the kitchen ". " Oh, my dear," said I—well, and just then came the note. A Miss Hawkins—that's all I know—a Miss Hawkins, of Bath. But, Mr. Knightley, how could you possibly have heard it? for the very moment Mr. Cole told Mrs. Cole of it, she sat down and wrote to me. A Miss Haw-kins——' "

Exercise 19

(a) Re-write the passage from *Cranford* making it as brief as possible without any loss of meaning.

(b) Reduce Miss Bates' speech to one sentence containing all that is really to the point.

(c) Correct the pleonasm, tautology or general verbosity of each of the following sentences :—

1. An annual grant is voted every year by Parliament. 2. The reluctant boy proceeded unwillingly to school because it was necessary that he should go thither. 3. *There's* a type of man that can't allow for a single moment that anybody should possess certain, what I may call, principles, and be prepared to argue in favour of these principles from early morn till dewy eve. Such is the base, the cowardly, the unmanly condition of that person there standing amongst your midst, that he can't recognise a honest 'eart when he meets one walking about. 4. He locked the door after he had previously seen that his prisoner was all right. 5. The guides rapidly made their way

downward along a narrow descending foot-
path. 6. You can enter this show free, gratis
and for nothing. 7. I put my hat upon my
head and walked into the Strand. 8. She is of
the same age as her twin brother. 9. He was
mounted on the top of a horse. 10. The defaulter was caused to enter a compartment in
the London train and so was conveyed to the
metropolis. 11. The birds filled the tree tops
with their morning song, making the air moist,
cool, and pleasant. 12. His elder brother was
his senior. 13. This incomparable picture cannot be compared with the others in that gallery.
14. If the picture is incomparable there is no
need to make the remark that it cannot be
compared.

LESSON XX

COMMON ERRORS

The number of ways in which writers go
wrong is legion, and no complete classification
of them can be made. But there are some
typical kinds of errors that occur so frequently
in composition that it is worth while giving
them special attention.

1. **Attraction.**—It frequently happens that
the nominative is separated from its verb by
several words. In this case we have a tendency
to make the verb agree with whichever subject
happens to be nearest it. " The misleading
power of the verse divisions—which seem to be
guides and are not—constantly betray him into
a difficulty."

Here the nominative is *power*, so the verb

should be *betrays*. This is a very natural yielding to the force of attraction of the nearer nouns *guides* and *divisions*. But it shows a clearer grip of the thought implied in a sentence when the writer proves by his very words that he keeps the grammatical subject in view. There is no ambiguity in saying that *A suite of rooms were engaged*, but it is better to make the verb agree with its singular nominative.

2. **Ellipses or Omissions.**—It is desirable to save words by proper ellipses. *He gave five books to his sister and three to his brother*. Here there is a gain rather than a loss from the omission of *books* after *three*. But it often happens that the omission covers an error. If the omitted word is inserted it is seen to be wrong, but when it is elided the implied blunder passes unnoticed. This occurs chiefly with prepositions.

" His objection and condoning of faults marked an ill-balanced judgment." Here we must insert *to* after *objection*. The same blunder is said to be made in the following :—

" Many sentences are miserably mangled, and the force of the emphasis totally lost."

It is maintained that the verb omitted after *emphasis* is *are* which is clearly ungrammatical. Many writers maintain that we are entitled to assume the right verb *is*, but it is better to err on the safe side and express the verb.

3. **The Loose Participle.**—A participle or participial phrase is naturally referred to the nearest nominative. If only one nominative is expressed, it claims all the participles that are not by the construction of the sentence

otherwise fixed. " Entering the house the door closed with a bang."

Here the nominative *door* claims the participle *entering*, which is clearly lying about loose. The meaning expressed is, *When the door entered the house the door closed with a bang*. The meaning intended is, *When I* (or he, or she, or it, or they, or John Smith) *entered the house, the door closed with a bang*.

Broken by distress and ill-health, I could do nothing to help the unfortunate fellow. As this sentence stands it is *I* who am broken, but the context in which it was found shows that it is " the unfortunate fellow " who is ill and distressed. Even in the improved form, *I could do nothing to help the unfortunate fellow, broken by distress and ill-health*, the participle is not quite securely fastened to the fellow. The words *who was* interpolated between *fellow* and *broken* prevent all possibility of mistake.

Sometimes the participle is said to be used absolutely. *A gun having gone off, the picket turned out. Our stores giving out, we thought it prudent to withdraw.* This use of the participle is permissible, as it is quite clear to which word the participle refers.

4. **The Split Infinitive.**—There is a growing tendency to place modifying words between the *to* and the remaining part of the infinitive, thus splitting the infinitive. *He was hardly able to even crawl*, should be . . . *even to crawl*. *To clumsily handle a musket* should be *to handle a musket clumsily*. So frequently is the infinitive now split in everyday writing that in a few years it may become permissible in good writing. It is better indeed to leave a split infinitive than

make a very obvious attempt to avoid it, as in this sentence—*The nations should combine to forbid flatly hostilities.* *To flatly forbid* is preferable to this distortion, but it would be best to re-model the sentence: *The nations should combine and should flatly forbid.* . . .[1]

5. *And* **with the Relative.**—*And* must never be used with the relative unless there be a parallel relative in the preceding clause. *There is a house on the hill, and which I have bought*, is so clearly wrong that one is ashamed to speak of the error : but experience shows that this error is quite common, particularly when sentences become long. *On the hill there is a house which I bought, and which I hope to occupy*, is correct. So is *I am a man who speaks the truth and fears no overlord.*

Certain Dangerous Words.—*Other* and *another.* These are what may be called boomerang words. They recoil upon us, and often make us say what we had no intention of saying. *We have no connection with the other quacks across the street* is not exactly what the shopkeeper meant. *Meanwhile my friend and another shady character proceeded to the pier* is clearly a bad sentence, though in the context in which it was used " my friend " did not really suffer ; for certain other shady characters had been spoken of in the previous sentence, and the *another* obviously referred to them. It is well, however, to make each sentence independent of contextual aid.

One.—The sort of impersonal use of this word in epigrammatic or proverbial saying (its gnomic use, as it is called) frequently leads to confusion.

[1] H. W. Fowler discusses the question very thoroughly, and very amusingly, in *Modern English Usage.*

If you begin with *one* you must keep on with *one* : you must not drop into *his*. *One must mind one's business if one wishes to succeed*. It is wrong to write, *One must mind his business if he wishes to succeed*. It is still worse to write, *One must mind their business if they wish to succeed*. *Any one*, on the other hand, does admit of *he, his* and *him*. *If any one guesses the truth he must not betray it*, or *let him not betray it*.

Only is perhaps the most ill-used word in the dictionary. Its grievance is that it is very often put in the wrong place.

I only cuffed him that time.

As this sentence stands it means : The only thing I did to him that time was to cuff him—that is, I did not kick him, or knock him down. But we may wish it to mean : I cuffed him on that one occasion only. This meaning is conveyed by putting the *only* just before *that time*. The rule is that *only* should always come immediately before the word or phrase it limits. As a matter of fact, in speaking we are able, by emphasis, to make it quite clear what we mean without changing the position of the *only* : but in writing we cannot depend on anything but the arrangement of the words.

Meaning indicated by emphasis.	Meaning indicated by arrangement.
1. I only *cuffed* him that time.	I only cuffed him that time
2. I only cuffed him *that time*.	I cuffed him only that time
3. I only cuffed *him* that time.	I cuffed only him that time
4. *I* only cuffed him that time.	Only I cuffed him that time

The word *alone* is often of service in easing

the work of *only*. Thus the meaning of the fourth sentence above could be most exactly expressed by *I alone cuffed him that time.* If we make a pause after *only*, it conveys a totally different meaning, as in the sentence : *I would follow your plan of pretending I did not object to his tricks, only, I cuffed him that time.* With *alone* this meaning is impossible.

This rule about placing adverbs immediately before the words they modify applies to other words besides *only*.

" Born in England, trained as a weaver, he had really wandered to America and the South Seas at the dictation of a restless and inquiring spirit."

Here *really* ought to come immediately before *at the dictation*. There is no question about the reality of his wandering.

Exercise 20

Correct the following sentences. The defects are not confined to those dealt with in the preceding lesson.

1. In every occurrence there are always some elements which are generally known or recognised by only a few. 2. It would be quite unfair if we read party newspapers and formed our opinions in unison with the opinions stated there. 3. Judged from this point of view, the picture may seem entirely different from a person who had been without the same knowledge. 4. We have no universal law to include under its sway everything. 5. They fall naturally into grooves which are smooth though well-worn. 6. The arguments may be perfectly logical of

each, and yet each arrives at a different result.
7. Progress would be impossible and our brains would be mere mechanism without reason.
8. We assume certain data known to be correct and consider the question in the light of this data. 9. He who has a complete and exhaustive knowledge of a subject is most likely to be correct. 10. The jury must be allowed to decide which is right and which is wrong. 11. Poor Paddy will alter his opinions, and see without shame that it was all for the best that Home Rule was denied them. 12. This will often prevent us from becoming too much prejudiced for or against any one particular conclusion. 13. This is the point at which we begin to enlighten any one to our views. 14. In discussion of any sort or thinking, the truth must be the goal towards which we strive. 15. Yet although two different opinions may be formed and may seem opposed to one another—yet on closer examination it sometimes happens that both are absolutely correct. 16. The newspaper man puts in a great many unnecessary details in order to add to his number of pennies per line. 17. The essentials of the story in each case is the same. 18. Conservative and Liberal Clubs, debating societies, and such institutions, have many good uses, social and otherwise, but none is more useful than the use which, in the second I have named, is the chief object of the society, namely debate. 19. There is no more difficult thing than to look at a subject from both sides of the question. 20. Seldom do we get many persons who think absolutely alike on a subject and never do we get any one who thinks exactly like his neighbour.

LESSON XXI

COMMON ERRORS—*continued*

He or she.—One of the most irritating inelegancies in English is the wooden insistence upon the alternatives *he or she* when dealing with a noun of common gender.

" The teacher must give his or her whole time to his or her professional duties; and if he or she undertakes extra professional duties a corresponding reduction will be made in his or her salary."

This is clumsy pedantry. A stocking may be made by a man, a woman or a machine; but we do not say, " If the maker of stockings is thorough in his, her or its work there will be no need for him, her or it to make provision for the immediate darning of weak places ".

An Act of Parliament now permits us to understand *he*, *his* and *him* in statutes as including *she*, *her* (or *hers*) and *her* respectively. We may therefore with a fair show of justice claim that the barbarous repetition of these alternatives shall from this date cease and determine. Talking of a class that is made up of women mainly, *she* may be made the standard. It is interesting to note, for example, that in America the pronoun corresponding to *teacher* is commonly *she*. But in all ordinary cases the authorised *he* should be preferred.

Broken Construction.—A very common vice in writing arises from carelessness. The end of the sentence forgets its beginning. It begins with one grammatical construction, and ends with another.

"Good principles, good temper and good manners will carry a man through the world much better than with the absence of either."

This is a hopeless sentence, take it how you will. The only thing that is clear about it is that *either* is wrong, whatever the sentence-maker meant. Did she mean the absence of any one of the three, or any two of them, or of the whole three? There is nothing to show. But for our present purpose the point is that the construction is broken at *than*: it should go on " he could be carried without them ". Or we may reconstruct the sentence from the latter part and make it read *The presence of good principles . . . will carry . . . than their absence.*

The Double Negative.—In the mathematical formula of the grammars, two negatives make an affirmative. *He was not allowed not to stay* is held to mean he was allowed to stay, whatever the man who made the sentence intended it to mean. Mistakes of this crude kind are seldom made, but some confusion arises by the occasional use of the double negative to convey a mild affirmative. *It is not impossible that I may be in town next week.* This is not liable to misconception, but the construction is not to be recommended. It frequently leads to confusion. Charles Lamb, speaking of Defoe's secondary novels, says : " It is impossible to believe while you are reading them, that a real person is not narrating to you everywhere nothing but what really happened to himself ". We have here three negatives, and nothing short of an algebraic equation can bring the meaning out straight. No writer is entitled to irritate his readers in this way, even though the meaning can be ultimately dug out of the clumsy construction.

A good deal of trouble arises from confusion in what is called the **sequence of tenses.** When two verbs depend on each other, their tenses must have a definite relation to each other. *I shall have much pleasure in accepting your kind invitation* is wrong, unless you really mean that just now you decline, though by-and-by you intend to accept; or unless you mean that you do accept now, though you have no pleasure in doing so, but look forward to be more pleased by-and-by.

I should have liked to have gone to see that play. Ask yourself the plain question : What is it that I " should have liked " to do? The plain, straightforward answer is—to go to see that play. To answer : to have gone to see that play would mean that at a certain moment you would have liked to be in the position of having gone to see that play. This is clearly not what you mean. You mean that at the moment *at* which you are speaking, you wish that at the moment *of* which you are speaking you had gone to see that play. *I should have liked* carries you back to the time at which you had the chance : once you are back at that time, the going to the play is a thing of the present.

If you are in doubt about any tenses of this kind your best plan is to carry yourself in thought back to the time in question, and use the tense you would *then* naturally use.

The difficulty that many experience in using

shall and **will** correctly arises from a confusion between two different kinds of futurity. In the first place there is what may be called the future of fate. Things that are going to happen will happen without our stir, or in spite of it. The person who describes things that must take place because of the nature of things, has clearly nothing to do with their happening beyond stating that they are going to happen. The following is the form in which this sort of futurity is expressed.

1.	I shall.	We shall.
2.	Thou wilt.	You will.
3.	He (she or it) will.	They will.

But sometimes the future does depend on the will of somebody, and then we have the future of will or the volitional future as it is called. The form for the volitional future is :—

1.	I will.	We will.
2.	Thou shalt.	You shall.
3.	He (she or it) shall.	They shall.

Notice particularly that the will upon which this future depends is not the will of *thou*, or *he*, or *she*, or *it*, or *you*, or *they*, but of the person who is writing or speaking. *You shall write two hundred lines*—here the will of the teacher prevails, not the will of the pupil whom he addresses. *Thou shalt not kill*—here God's will dominates the future, not ours to whom the command is addressed.

If we say to one who has ill-treated us *You will repent of this*, we mean that things are so arranged in this world that sooner or later those who do ill have cause to repent. But if we say *You shall repent it,* we mean that we intend to take active measures to secure the repentance.

Take the case of a wet day and examine the following correct statements of the future : You will get wet if you do not put up your umbrella. I shall get wet if I do not put up my umbrella. I will get wet rather than put up my umbrella. He will get wet if he does not put up his umbrella. He shall get wet if my service demands it. You shall put up your umbrella, for I cannot afford to buy you a new hat.

The **first personal pronoun** should not too often be used in general writing. Its proper place is in passages where you are stating a view that is not generally held, and that is likely to meet with opposition, and in familiar forms of composition it is permissible. Never introduce it by way of apology. *In my opinion, so far as I can see, it appears to me,* are all unnecessary, since they are implied in the fact that you are writing at all.

Exercise 21

State what is wrong with each of the following sentences, and show how to improve them :—

1. The lion made a gracious bow to his hostess and said that there had not been at a better gathering since the time of Noah's Ark. 2. After thinking for a long time a bright idea struck her. 3. "Five score guests !" she said to herself, "where will I get food for them all?" 4. I called upon the editor and wished to have

submitted my manuscript to him. 5. Regard is to be had to every one's circumstances, healths and abilities. 6. Five score were no joke to feed. 7. Unlike all the other beasts of the forest the fish could not accept the ant's invitation. 8. The accused neither admitted the charge nor did he not deny it. 9. After enjoying the day in dancing and frolicking all thoughts turned towards supper. 10. The admiration of this poem was unanimous. 11. For want of debt he died in poverty. 12. We admit the gift's generosity, but the Town Council in accepting it will, we believe, be found to have saddled themselves with a white elephant. 13. Paris is larger than any city in France. 14. I am one of those who cannot describe what I do not see. 15. Put one of the pills in a little water and swallow it three times daily before meals. 16. She has a bad habit of procrastinating everything till to-morrow. 17. The sparring with words between Beatrice, who says " nobody marks you " and yet she herself does, and Benedick made us wonder how all that will end. 18. Little Hop-o'-my-thumb was the cleverest of all his brothers. 19. The old woman who received the coin was mother of the girl whose marriage all these years she had come between. 20. There was nothing for it but to let her have her wish, and, if possible, to aid her towards the consummation of it.

LESSON XXII

PARAPHRASING

When we take a passage, examine it carefully so as to grasp its meaning, and then try to express that meaning in another form, we are said to paraphrase the passage. It is plain that several of the exercises we have already worked are really examples of paraphrasing. When, for example, we express in literal terms what was before expressed in a figure of speech, we are paraphrasing.

There is a great difference of opinion about the value of paraphrasing as an exercise in composition. As used in schools there is certainly a great deal to be said against it. An especially good passage is chosen from an especially good author, and the pupil is invited to express its meaning in other words. Now, in a selected passage from a selected author we may assume that the best words and the most suitable constructions have been employed. Accordingly, we find the pupil forced to content himself with words and constructions that are not the best. The most that intelligent and assiduous students can hope for, is to succeed in selecting the second-best modes of expression.

That there is a great deal of truth in this objection no one who has had experience in marking paraphrasing exercises will deny. But it must not be forgotten that there are compensating advantages. The exercise demands a careful examination of the passage to be paraphrased. This has the same value for the student of letters that dissection has for the student of medicine. In both cases, no doubt, the subject is spoiled, but much has been learned in the spoiling. Further, the very badness of the version produced by the student increases his appreciation of the model. It may be said that a student can learn nothing by writing poor English. To this it is enough to reply that he may at least learn that it is poor English. An exercise in composition is not to be tested by the quality of the work produced at the time, but by the effect upon the student. After all, the written exercise itself finds its way into the waste-paper basket : the effect of having written it remains with him.

All the same, we naturally want the English used to be as good as possible in the circumstances. We must therefore guard against some common errors in paraphrasing. The first of these is the belief that every word of the original must be changed. This produces such abortions as *the bovine race* for *cattle*, and *lacteal fluid* for *milk*. In paraphrasing, the dictionary must be very cautiously used. The exercise should consist in reading and understanding the passage set, taking it all in, assimilating it, making it our own, and then expressing it in our own way with the least possible change in meaning or tone. Those who seek to dig the meaning out of a dictionary will produce something like the following which was handed in by a dull boy of sixteen. The passage is from Scott. Speaking of James IV. allowing Surrey to cross the Till unopposed, the poet asks :—

> But why stands Scotland idly now,
> Dark Flodden, on thy airy brow?

The paraphrase ran, *But why does Scotland hold herself upright at the present moment on the atmospherical forehead of black Flodden ?* The proper rendering in good second-rate English would be : *But why do the Scottish forces still remain inactive on the breezy heights of gloomy Flodden ?* The original contains two figures of speech. *Scotland* is metonymy, *dark Flodden* is apostrophe : both are omitted in the paraphrase, for it is a recognised rule that we must not seek to carry our figures over from the original. Not infrequently we meet phrases that defy paraphrasing as they stand. We must not take the phrase, or even the sentence, as the unit of paraphrasing, but the whole passage. This enables us so to change the whole structure as to preserve the complete meaning, while avoiding literal renderings of individual phrases. *Motherly dove* is a phrase of this kind. We may insinuate the idea somewhere in a passage, but we cannot carry the phrase over bodily without disaster. No sentence, however skilful, could redeem *maternal pigeon*.

It is to be remembered that paraphrasing does not necessarily mean changing from first-class to second-class English. The custom of the school has rather favoured the assumption that paraphrasing can act in only one direction—from good to bad. Take the following example from a book whose purpose is not primarily educational. The magistrate asks the accused :—

" ' Is it a fact, my girl, that you absconded from your situation ? '

" Mord Em'ly requested the sergeant to translate the question, and the sergeant complied.

Did she do a bunk from the shop her mother got for her?

" ' You may take it at that,' replied Mord Em'ly gruffly. ' Please yourself.'

" ' It seems to me that we must look on you as incorrigible.'

" The sergeant obliged again. ' His worship says that you're a bad nut.' "

As a matter of fact Mord Em'ly had not been in a shop, but in a house as domestic servant, yet *shop* is none the less an excellent paraphrase, for in Em'ly's language it is inexactly equivalent to *situation*. The *bad nut* paraphrase, again, is quite accurate. It is to be noted that the author makes the sergeant *translate*, but from our point of view *paraphrase* would be a better word, as the meaning has not to be transferred from one language to another, but only from one form of English to another. From the point of view of the author of the passage quoted, however, *translate* is the better word, as he wishes to impress the fact that Em'ly and the magistrate really speak two different languages. In fact *translate* is here a figure of speech—hyperbole.

Real translation is indeed one of the best ways of practising composition. The ideas are supplied in a clear and intelligible form, and yet neither the words nor the constructions of the English version are anticipated. If you know a little of any other language than English you should *write out* every week an English version of a page or so from that other language. The passage need not be a difficult one, as it is not a test of knowledge of French or Latin or

German, but an exercise in the use of English to express given ideas.

Turning passages written in dialect into standard English is another useful exercise in paraphrasing, for you have to find equivalents for dialect words and very often to use different constructions.

In translating, students are frequently at a loss whether they should adopt a literal or a free rendering of the passage set. A literal rendering is useful as indicating a clear grasp of the grammatical structure of the language from which the translation is made. Teachers of foreign languages are naturally inclined to favour a literal rendering, particularly at the early stages of studying a language. At later stages the free translation is to be preferred. The real test of a good translation is the degree in which it conveys to the reader the same impression as the original conveys to one who is master of the original language. *To do a bunk* is not a literal translation of *to abscond*, but it meant for Em'ly exactly what the big verb meant for the magistrate.

The paraphrasing of fine passages of poetry is seldom well done. The logical meaning may be accurately conveyed, but the tone of the passage is so different that the real meaning is lost. In dealing with poetry the *literal* rendering is nearly always wrong. This is particularly the case where numbers are concerned—*Half a league, half a league, half a league onward,* does not mean quite the same thing as *a league and a half,* while *four and a half miles* is still farther from the original.

Besides conveying exactly the same impression as the original, a translation should not read like a translation : it should not suggest the language from which it has come, but should read exactly as if the ideas had come straight from the mind of the writer, without the intervention of another language. So with paraphrasing—when finished it should read like a bit of original composition. It must express the meaning of the original, but it must do this without sacrificing its claim to be good ordinary idiomatic English. This is a case where the method of testing by time is specially useful. A paraphrase should always be judged by the effect it produces as English, when read after time has been allowed for the original to pass from the memory.

There is one great advantage connected with the practice of paraphrasing. It enforces the widening of the student's vocabulary. We all fall into ruts in our use of words. If we write a letter or an essay we are at liberty to choose our own words, and we naturally fall back upon those we are familiar with. In this way our stock of available words tends to remain fixed. In paraphrasing, the very fact that a certain number of words and phrases are already used, sets us seeking farther afield for others. Further, since the ideas expressed are not our own, it is probable that our familiar words do not fit them so well as they do our own familiar thoughts, so that again we are forced to call in words from our reading vocabulary, and in many cases these are added to our permanent writing vocabulary.

In dealing with the following passages set

for paraphrase it will be worth your while to attend to the following rules :—

1. Read over the passage carefully two or three times to get a clear grasp of the meaning of the whole and the inter-relations of the parts. If need be, turn up any doubtful words in your dictionary, not so much to find equivalents as to make sure of the meaning of the passage.

2. Having made the matter your own, consider carefully in what form it can be most suitably expressed. If it is poetry it will be necessary to give your paraphrase an elevated tone. Do not try to write what is sometimes called prose poetry : let your prose be plain prose, but in this case certain familiar words and constructions cannot be admitted.

3. The tone is the only thing that *must* be preserved. The general form may be completely changed. The original may be highly figurative, the paraphrase severely literal.

4. Paraphrasing is not so exacting as the police court which demands the truth, the whole truth and nothing but the truth. It does not rigidly insist on the middle demand. Details, if they have not an important bearing on the main subject, need not be reproduced, or may have different but parallel details introduced in their place. The writer is left free here, so long as the details in the paraphrase give the same background effect as the details in the original. The "nothing but the truth" is rigidly exacted. No important idea must appear in the paraphrase unless it appears in the original.

5. When the paraphrase has been written out, leave it for a day or two, and then take it up and read it through apart from any consideration of the original, merely to see if it reads like English.

Exercise 22

Paraphrase the following passages :—

(a) I'll get this juggler, if he quits him well,
   An audience here as choice as can be lured.
   For me, when a poor devil does his best,
   'Tis my delight to soothe his soul with praise.
   What though the best be bad? remains the good
   Of throwing food to a lean hungry dog.
   I'd give up the best jugglery in life
   To see a miserable juggler pleased.
   But that's my humour. Crowds are malcontent
   And cruel as the Holy —— Shall we go?
   All of us now together?

(b) In this case give two paraphrases, a close one and a free.

It is a notable tale, that old Syr Roger Chamloe, sometime chiefe Justice, wold tell of himselfe. When he was Auncient [Senior Barrister] in Inne of Courte, certaine yong Ientlemen were brought before him, to be corrected for certain misorders : And one of the lustiest saide : Syr, we be yong ientlemen, and wise men before vs, haue proued all facion and yet those haue done full well : this they said, because it was well knowen, that Syr Roger had bene a good feloe in his yougth. But he aunswered them verie wiselie. In deede saith he, I was, as you are now : and I had twelue feloes like vnto my self, but not one of them came to a good ende. And therfore, folow not my example in yougth, but folow my councell in aige, if ever ye thinke to cum to his place, or to thies yeares, that I am cum vnto, lesse ye meete either with pouertie or Tiburn in the way.

(c) Our amusements for the fortnit we stopt here were boath numerous and daliteful; nothink, in fact, could be more *pickong*, as they say. In the morning before breakfast, we boath walked on the Peer; master in a blue mareen jackit, and me in a slap-up new livry; both provided with long sliding opra-glasses, called as I said (I don't know Y, but I spose it's a scientafick term) tallowscoops. With these we igsamined, very attentively the otion, the seaweed, the pebbils, the dead cats, the fishwimmin, and the waives (like little children playing at leap-frog), which came tumbling over I another on to the shoar. It seemed to me as if they were scrambling to get there, as well they might, being sick of the sea, and anxious for the blessid, peaceable *terry firmy*.

After brexfast, down we went again (that is, master on his beat, and me on mine—for my place in this foring town was a complete *shinycure*), and putting our tallyscoops again in our eyes, we egsamined a little more the otion, pebbils, dead cats, and so on; and this lasted till dinner, and dinner lasted till bed-time, and bed-time lasted till nex day, when came brexfast, and dinner, and tally-scooping, as befoar.

This is the way with all people of this town, of which, as I've heard say, there is ten thousand happy English, who lead this plesnt life from year's end to year's end.

(d) " Weel, the presbytery be't," says I, for I saw that my wife's patience, never verra lang at the best, was comin' near an end. I ken the length o't to a hair as by this time I hae a good richt to do. " Weel, the coort met an' was constitutit."

" What's that ? " asked Bob Adair.

" Fegs, I do not ken, ye'll hae to ask the clerk, it was him that said it," says I, " an' then there was reports, an' strings o' feegures like laddies' coonts [sums]; but naebody payed muckle attention, but talkit to their neebours till the clerk caaed ' Order ! ' Then they were quaite for half a meenit, an' syne at it again. Deed the clerk talkit too when he didna mind."

" Deer sirce, 'an that's a presbytery. I thocht it was like a week o' sacraments ! " said my wife.

" Verra far frae that," says I, " for o' a' the craiturs to fecht, doos an' ministers are the maist quarrelsome."

" Did oor minister fecht ? " asked the mistress, verra pointed.

" Na, he was raither a peacemaker, so to speak," says I cautious like ; " of coorse a man haes whiles to speak his mind."

" Ow ! he's the wee white hen that never lays away, oor minister, I ken," says she, dried like.

" Ye never war the bird to fyle yer ain kirk riggin," said Rob. Whiles I'm feared that auld Rob is gettin' a wee doited.

LESSON XXIII

PRÉCIS-WRITING

In paraphrasing you have to re-cast a given passage in your own words. In writing a précis, or summary, you go further, for you have to re-cast a given passage in the smallest number of words possible. Précis-writing is frequently used for official purposes, when a summary of letters or documents must be prepared for an official who has no time to read the originals; but there are many other occasions when it is useful to be able to express a number of ideas in the smallest possible space, and practice in précis-writing will help you to form a clear concise style.

In condensing ten pages of print into two or three, it is clear that much must be omitted. The art of précis-writing lies in making the right omissions, and in skilfully combining what is left. We may take certain general rules as a guide :—

(1) Omit all matters that have no bearing on the general topic—and all details that are merely picturesque, e.g. *Princess —— was bareheaded and wore a sealskin coat, when she visited the hospital.* . . .

(2) When two or more subjects, more or less distinct, are discussed, keep them in separate paragraphs.

(3) Use indirect speech.

(4) Be simple, concise and direct. Avoid repetition. E.g. *He wrote a letter in which he*

gave the Prime Minister the information that . . . would become : *The Prime Minister was informed that.* . . . Omit all metaphorical expressions, or, if they are necessary in the summary, replace them by plainer terms.

(5) Use your own words as a rule. A précis which is made up of words and phrases borrowed from the original will in most cases not be clear to anyone who has not read the original. (You must of course keep the most important words of the original.)

It is an excellent exercise to condense a longish essay by stages. Take an essay of some dozen pages, and try to express its substance in eight pages, then in six, then in four, in two, in one, and finally in half a page. You will find that you do not omit equally throughout the essay. More goes at one point than at another. Three pages may be reduced to a dozen lines, while some pages can hardly be reduced by a third. The essential thing is to retain the really important points, and to arrange them according to their value in the essay. The great advantage of thus making abstracts of long compositions is the training it gives in the discrimination of the various parts in their relation to the whole, and in this way you will cultivate a feeling for proportion.

The following is a specially useful exercise for two students working together. Let each choose an essay of about a dozen pages, and reduce it to a précis of about one page. Let them exchange their précis. Then let each elaborate the other's précis into an essay of about six pages, and condense his own twelve-page essay into a six-page précis. The interest lies in comparing the six-page essays on the same subject. For in each pair one is a précis of a twelve-page essay, and the other an elaboration of a single-page précis. For example, A condenses a twelve-page essay on Capital Punishment into one page : B does the same for an essay of the same length on Fox-hunting into six, and B expands A's one page of Capital Punishment into six. Next A condenses his twelve pages of Capital Punishment into six, and B does the like with his Fox-hunting. If A's six-page abstract on Capital Punishment agrees in essentials with B's six-page elaboration on the same subject, it may be fairly assumed that both A and B have appreciated and maintained the relative importance of the different elements of the essays. If the two versions differ materially, they offer a capital field for discussion, which cannot fail to train both students in the perception of proportion in literary style.

Excellent examples of this process of précis-writing are to be found in our daily newspapers. The little paragraphs over the leading articles usually express very clearly the substance of several columns in the middle of the paper. You cannot do better than turn from the three-column report of some political meeting to the quarter-column paragraph over the leader. In most cases you will be sorry you read the three columns.

Exercise 23

As an exercise in abstract-making, give the substance of the following passage in as few words as you can, without omitting anything essential.

" It is asserted by Horace, that ' if matter be once got together, words will be found with very little difficulty '; a position which though sufficiently plausible to be inserted in poetical precepts, is by no means strictly and philosophically true. If words were naturally and necessarily consequential to sentiments it would always follow, that he who has most knowledge must have most eloquence, and that every man would clearly express what he fully understood : yet we find, that to think, and discourse, are often the qualities of different persons: and many books might surely be produced where just and noble sentiments are degraded and obscured by unsuitable diction. Words, therefore, as well as things, claim the care of an author. Indeed of many authors, and those not useless or contemptible, words are almost the only care : many make it their study, not so much to strike out new sentiments, as to recommend those which are already known to more favourable notice by fairer decorations : but every man, whether he copies or invents, whether he delivers his own thoughts or those of another, has often found himself deficient in the power of expression, big with ideas which he could not utter, obliged to ransack his memory for terms adequate to his conceptions, and at last unable to impress upon his reader the image existing in his own mind. It is one of the common distresses of a writer, to be within a word of a happy period, to want only a single epithet to give amplification its full force, to require only a correspondent term in order to finish a paragraph with elegance, and make one of its members answer to the other : but these deficiencies cannot always be supplied : and after a long study and vexation, the passage is turned anew, and the web unwoven that was so nearly finished. But when thoughts and words are collected and adjusted, and the whole composition at last concluded, it seldom gratifies the author when he comes coolly and deliberately to review it, with the hopes which had been excited in the fury of the performance : novelty always captivates the mind; as our thoughts rise fresh upon us, we readily believe them just and original, which, when the pleasure of production is over, we find to be mean and common, or borrowed from the works of others, and supplied by memory rather than invention."

LESSON XXIV

COMPOSITION—FINDING MATERIAL

In earlier exercises you have been asked to write short compositions, but the matter has in most cases been suggested for your use. In this lesson we shall consider the problem of collecting material and expressing it in a suitable form.

Your attitude to this problem will depend on yourself. You may find that, when you are faced with a subject on which to write, your ideas come tumbling out in such profusion that when you come to set them down you hardly know where to begin. In despair, you take the first that comes, and let the others follow in what order they will. The result is a rich disorder, in which significant and insignificant facts jostle together, and no clear argument can be discerned. If you have to write an essay or description, your best plan is to write down all your ideas, as they come, on a piece of rough paper. When you have finished, go through them carefully, striking out whatever is irrelevant to the main theme. (How you are to decide which facts are irrelevant, we shall discuss later.) Then go through your list once more, this time grouping the facts which are connected with each other, and arranging the groups so that one group naturally leads on to the next. Your material is thus sorted and you are now almost ready to begin your essay.

You may, on the other hand, find that when you are faced with a subject for an essay or description, your ideas will not come. The virgin blankness of your paper paralyses your mind; you write down the title and can write no more. Your case is worse at first sight than that of the student with too much to say. You could write a brilliant essay, wittily expressed, elegantly arranged—if only you had something to say in it. Your difficulty is more than half psychological. You are like the nervous guest at a party who can say nothing until he has been drawn out by skilful questioning. For such a one, the question and answer method will prove the most stimulating, in essay-writing as in conversation. But you yourself must ask the questions, and how are you to find them?

Let us take a concrete example. Suppose you are asked to write an essay on your favourite season of the year, then your first instinctive question will be—" How to decide? " To this there is the obvious answer : your choice will depend (1) on the weather; (2) on the way you spend your leisure (for this will clearly be more affected by the weather than your regular work). The first point suggests the obvious question : what kind of weather do you like best? When you have decided this, you will be able to expand your answer into a more detailed description. The second point suggests two more questions : (1) what are your favourite leisure occupations? (2) to what season are they suited? The answers to these questions may also be developed at length. If, for example, your favourite pastime is bathing, then you can describe the pleasures of bathing on a hot day (in sea or river or pool), the delicious coolness that follows your bathe, or the pleasures of sunbathing afterwards. Thus one question has led on to another, until you end with ample material for your essay, and you have the advantage over the quicker student in that your ideas are then arranged in a logical order. Whether the subject of your essay is simple, like this one, or demands more thought, the important part is to find a leading question, and the rest will follow of their own accord.

If you are asked for plain description, your questions will be different. If you have to describe a concrete object, you may begin by asking : What does it look like, in colour, shape, size? What is its use? What associations has it for me? Or, if you are describing a person : What does he look like? What do I know of his character, way of living? What is his use and importance? These are general questions, but they can be modified to suit the needs of the subject. When you have practised this method several times, it will be easy to find questions, and you will ask and answer them almost unconsciously.

But your work is not yet over. As you gain practice in collecting ideas, you will find that you have too many ideas to fit into a single essay, and that they differ too widely to fit into an orderly scheme. You cannot express every view on the subject given, and you have doubtless unconsciously adopted a single point of view. Yet you will be wise nevertheless to look through your material, and consider whether all your ideas are consistent. If, for instance, you are writing an essay condemning capital punishment, you must not say at one point that the death penalty is a survival of barbarism, and later aver that it is still necessary in a civilised community. If you are unable to make up your mind, then you must make it clear from the beginning that you are going to examine both sides of the question. Even if you can find no inconsistencies in your material, pruning may still be necessary, and all irrelevancies must be cut away. You may class as irrelevant all that does not enlighten or explain or expand your main argument. We all recognise irrelevancy in conversation, and Jane Austen has caricatured it in the person of Miss Bates.[1] It is almost as easy to be garrulous and irrelevant in writing as in conversation, especially if you have a gift for writing fluently. To decide what is irrelevant, you must put your-

_____
[1] In *Emma*, see p. 112.

self in the position of your reader, and think what he expects to find in your work. He may come to you for exact and useful knowledge. In that case your description or your argument must be clear in outline and exact in detail, and all that is fanciful or in any way personal must be left out. He may, on the other hand, come to you for entertainment, wishing to receive your impressions or reflections in a pleasant form. In that case, you must strike out all that is obvious and uninteresting. You must not begin an essay on a railway terminus with the definition : " A railway terminus is a place from which trains begin and at which they end their journeys ". Your task is to please, and such bald facts are as out of place in such an essay as they would be in polite conversation. In short, your final tests in selecting material, as in all other problems of writing, must be the question : Is this appropriate ?

Exercise 24

Prepare the material for a short general essay on a big railway station.

LESSON XXV

DESCRIPTION

Description, as was shown in the last lesson, may be of two kinds. You may write a plain, exact description, designed to give practical information, or you may write a general description with no other purpose than to entertain. Persons with any gift for writing will usually find the second kind of description easier than the first; for them exercises in plain description are very useful, since they demand clear accurate writing, and clearness and accuracy are virtues which imaginative people often forget to cultivate.

It is to be remembered that the value of a description depends upon the combined work of two persons. The writer really analyses mentally the thing to be described, and places the parts in what he considers the most suitable order before the reader, who must in turn try to reconstruct these parts into the whole with which the writer started. In describing scenery, for example, the writer mentions that there was a mountain here, a stream there, a certain tree or group of trees elsewhere, and so on. He probably uses an adjective or two about each object, and certain prepositions and adverbs of direction. From these indications the reader dips into his own storehouse of ideas, selects mountains, streams, and trees that seem to fit the case, and combines them in such a way as not to contradict any of the prepositions or adverbs. The result is a mental picture which coincides sufficiently with the author's mental picture to allow of author and reader each using his own picture as a background for what follows.

It is good practice to try to describe some practical process to a friend to whom it is unfamiliar, and to see how far he can understand it from your description. When you can accurately describe a process such as touch-typing or handweaving, or can give clear directions for reaching a certain meeting-place, then you will know that your style has gained accuracy and precision. Mrs. Beeton's cookery book might serve as a model for this kind of writing. Clearness and conciseness are essential in a recipe, and Mrs. Beeton had both these virtues. Her secret is that like all good cooks, she thought clearly and methodically. In practising this style you will do well to follow her example.

In describing a scene or a background, you will need a different technique, but your practice in exact description will have done you good service. Detailed description is now somewhat out of fashion : few modern novels begin with a lengthy description of the house in which the hero was born. It is recognised that such exact detail does not necessarily make the scene more vivid, and that a few clear touches are more effective and put less strain on the reader.

Yet the writer must not thereby save himself trouble. He may be content to say that his hero was born in " a low white house with a cedar tree leaning over it ", but he must himself know much more about it. He must have peeped into all the rooms, he must know the position of the pantry, and whether the drawing-room has a french window. It is only when he sees the house clearly in his imagination that he can select the points that are important to his reader. He must not make up the details as he goes along : such a feckless method betrays itself, and will render the background of the story unconvincing and unsubstantial. Jane Austen, it is said, worked with a map before her showing the imaginary village in which her novel was set, with the houses in which the characters lived, clearly marked upon it. Her imaginary world was thus made real; everything that happened in it was credible, because correct in detail. Even if you do not draw a map, you should imitate Jane Austen in getting the background clear in your head before you begin to write.

Let us assume, then, that you have followed this method. Your imaginary country is mapped; you know precisely the number of bedrooms in your imaginary house, and have decided the colour of the drawing-room curtains. Now, all this detail must be pushed back into a corner of your mind. Imagine the scene now in its entirety and pick out the details which will be most vivid to your reader. " A low white house with a cedar tree leaning over it. . . ." Perhaps that is enough for the present, yet, if the house is to play an important part in your story, you may perhaps say a little more, something like this perhaps: " It was a low white house, standing back from the road; its green front door opened on to a small neat garden, and its windows were darkened by a great cedar tree."

You will ask, perhaps, how you are to decide which details are to be selected, which forgotten. It is impossible to make general rules, but three suggestions may be given. You must, of course, give some general features that the readers' imagination may have something to work on. These will be obvious—trees, river, houses and the rest—you can describe nothing without giving some definite features such as these. Next in importance is colour, for this is very easy to carry in the mind; given one or two colours, the imagination can create a picture in bold outline. Lastly, you may add whatever details are unusual or arresting (like the cedar tree in the example given). If you are interested in this kind of description, you should notice very carefully the descriptions given in any good novels, noting what is included and what left out. Then try yourself to describe some well-known place or scene—your own house—for example—choosing the details which would make it vivid to a stranger.

Exercise 25

(a) For practice do as many of the following descriptions as your knowledge permits. The two fundamental rules to be attended to are : (1) Assume nothing on the part of your reader but a fair knowledge of English and a moderate amount of common sense. (2) Pay special attention to the order in which you present matters. In describing a process it is well to take the different parts in the order in which they actually occur. For example, in describing how to fumigate a green-house it is too late to remark when the description is half finished : " Close all the ventilators ".

The Process of	Instruments.
Cyclostyling.	A pair of opera-glasses.
Folding table-napkins.	A roll-top desk.
Fumigating a green-house.	A trouser-stretcher.
Propelling a boat with one oar.	A fountain-pen.
Mounting a bicycle.	A cyclometer.
Preparing a salad-dressing.	An automobile.
Driving at golf.	A pianola.
Focusing in photography.	An hour-glass.

149

(*b*) " For Sale : Country cottage, one reception, 3 bedrooms, kitchen, bath, h. and c., all modern conveniences, old-world garden with lily pond. Apply Dodger & Dodger, House-agents, Dumbleditch."

Using this house-agents' description as a guide, imagine what the country cottage might really look like, and then describe it, pretending that your description is part of a story.

LESSON XXVI

NARRATIVE

In Lesson XXIV no mention was made of collecting material for narrative. It must be assumed that you have the material for your story in your head, or you would not be sitting down to write it. Your problem is to decide what is to be omitted, what briefly told, and how you are to arrange the material that is left.

The arrangement of matter is to a large extent imposed from without. Things happen in a certain order, and in most cases the narrator should follow that order. It is true that in dealing with a long series of events, as in history or in an epic poem, it may be necessary to present various incidents rather in the order of importance than in the exact order in which they occurred. Epics almost never begin at the beginning : they start off in the middle of an interesting situation and go on, gradually picking up preceding events as the story develops. The same is true of many novels.

On the other hand, many narratives, such as *Robinson Crusoe* and *The Pilgrim's Progress*, follow the time order : they begin at the beginning and go right on.

Even in those cases where series of events are grouped according to their importance in the whole narrative, the events within each series must be given in their time order. It would appear, therefore, that once the general arrangement of series is made, the rest is a mere matter of memory. You start at the beginning of each series, and let the mind recall each event as it happened. But the matter is not quite so easy as it looks. Two opposite lines of error present themselves : we may omit essential points, or we may include points that have no value in the narrative.

Listen to children telling stories. One of the commonest remarks you will hear is " Oh, but I forgot to tell you that . . .". This is said when the child finds that the development of the story demands a knowledge of some preceding incident, that at an earlier part of the narrative was not of sufficient consequence to command his attention. On the other hand, when we listen to the stories of certain garrulous persons we are not spared a single detail, however unimportant.

The true view is that here as elsewhere we must make a selection among the facts that present themselves, we must choose only those that are of consequence in respect of the purpose we have at the time. The reader of a narrative is entitled to assume that every fact set forth does something towards aiding the development of the story. For example, if we are told that a man walked to town " by the nearest way ", we have a right to assume that he was in a hurry to get there. If the context shows that there was no need for haste, then we are justified in assuming that later on in the story we shall find that something depended on his taking this particular way to town. Sometimes, it is true, a remark is introduced not for its own sake, or for future use, but merely to convey a present impression. *I heard the click of Aunt Maria's knitting needles* need not lead us to expect those needles to play a prominent part in the story. The context shows that the reference is made in order to strengthen the impression of the silence that reigned at a critical moment in the story.

While in narrative there is thus the usual need for a point of view and for a corresponding selection of material, there is always the great help of the time order. You must choose the proper incidents, but the incidents all pass through your mind in the order in which they originally occurred. In description, on the other hand, the facts may present themselves to the mind in any order. We must adopt our point of view, and then determine the relative importance of the facts at our disposal. It is true that, speaking generally, we have in description all the facts arranged according to space, as in a narrative they are arranged according to time. We may describe emotions, theories and other immaterial things, but the beginner in description will do well to confine himself to things seen, and there he has the aid of space arrangement. Even with this limitation he has to determine which facts are, for his present purpose, the most suitable to begin with.

Your treatment of the facts will be decided in part by your method of telling the story. The most usual method is to pretend that the author knows everything and is everywhere. In telling the story he can enter the minds of the characters and proclaim their secret thoughts; he can describe what happened in one place, and afterwards what was happening at the same time in another; he can traverse infinite distance, and leap across the years. This method is clearly most convenient since it imposes no restraint upon the writer, but there are times when other methods are appropriate.

When a story deals very particularly with the experience of a single character, it is common to make that character the narrator, and to write in the first person. *David Copperfield* and *Robinson Crusoe* are examples of this method. It has certain limitations in that you can only present what the narrator himself heard or saw or experienced, but it is often a more convincing method, since the reader easily imagines himself in the place of the character who is telling the story.

A third method is to make an imaginary character tell the story for you—a difficult method, which should not be attempted by the inexperienced. It is often used when the story would be incredible if told in a more direct form. Reading it, you feel that the author is not vouching for the truth himself, but heard it from another, who possibly heard it from a third. Henry James uses it very brilliantly in his ghost story *The Turn of the Screw*, where the events would seem utterly beyond belief if the story were told more directly. Many ghosts stories

153

employ this method. It is used with different effect when the narrator is a " character " like W. W. Jacobs' night watchman,[1] for then much of the fun of the story lies in the way it is told. " Q " uses all three methods in a very skilful way in a short story, *The Roll-call of the Reef*.[2] It opens in the first person, with a conversation between the author and his host, but this merely serves as introduction. His host tells a ghost story, which he himself heard from his father, and because he is telling a story well-known to him he uses the freer direct method as if he himself were the author. He thus reaps the advantages of all three methods. You will be well advised not to try any such intricate methods of story-telling yourself, but you will learn very much from studying how they are handled by accomplished writers.

Exercise 26

For practice in narrative give an account of the Adventures of a Shilling, as told by itself. Make up your mind before you start, (*a*) when your shilling began its life, (*b*) which incidents in its life you consider worth narrating, (*c*) what is its present state. You may include a long or a short period, but you should try to account for the whole period you have chosen, even though great parts of it were spent in uninteresting ways. The dull parts should be indicated, the interesting parts told fully.

[1] *Captains All* and other volumes.
[2] From *Wandering Heath*.

LESSON XXVII

LETTER-WRITING

Letter-writing is the freest of all forms of composition and probably the pleasantest. You may feel self-conscious in writing an essay or an exercise, but a letter is an extension of conversation, a substitute for speech. Those who find essay-writing too formal will find it the best medium, for a letter is the converse of an essay in that the less you think about it the better it will be. Naturalness and ease are its chief essentials, and these must come unconsciously, if they come at all. The best letters are written for an immediate purpose, and destined for the waste-paper basket as soon as that purpose is fulfilled. Once you begin to think of a letter as a piece of literary work its charm vanishes—a warning that is less necessary to-day than it has been in the past when a young man could send his friend the earnest injunction—" Remember to put my letters in a book, *neatly* ".[1]

Since letters are really conversations by post, the nearer they approach the freedom of conversation the better. That is the charm of Charles Lamb's letters—that they give this illusion of talk, so that reading them you can hear in fancy all the changes in his voice. This intimacy is the essence of good letter-writing. Its secret is beyond analysis, yet two ingredients are clear—simplicity and appropriateness. Your aim must be to produce the simplicity of con-

[1] Boswell, Dr. Johnson's chronicler, writing to his friend, Temple.

versation without its flatness. You are free in a letter to use the colloquialisms and the looser constructions of speech (provided you respect the rules of grammar), but you must avoid the pitfalls of excessive simplicity. You must use the arts of style, but use them unobtrusively. The banalities which pass unnoticed in conversation are glaring when written down. If you write of an experience, you must make it as vivid to your correspondent as it is to yourself. If you write of a book or a play, your opinion must be sensible and persuasive.

The interest of your letter will depend very much on its appropriateness. Since your reader is chiefly to be considered, you must write on matters which interest him. A letter which differs from an essay only in beginning " Dear—" and ending " Yours affectionately " does not deserve the name. Your business in a letter is not only to express yourself, but to express your relationship to the person to whom you are writing. Let not your friends say of you, as Queen Victoria said of Mr. Gladstone : " He addresses me as if I were a public meeting ! "

Clearly the manner is more important than the matter, and some of the best letters in the world have been written on the lightest of subjects. If you write naturally, simply, and appropriately, then your letters are sure to be pleasant. The following extract from a young lady's letter is a happy example of this kind of writing, though she[1] has no claim whatever to literary pretensions. She has been sea-bathing— a bold adventure in 1792 :

" We had a nice dip : the machines are very

[1] Louisa Holroyd.

convenient with a curtain all round so that nobody can see you. You are not put in as at Brighton, only one woman gives you her hand and in you jump. Aunt and I went in two machines, but close together, so she had the satisfaction of hearing me flounce in, and I of hearing how she behaved as the same woman executed us both."

A very ordinary passage, you may say—loosely constructed, badly punctuated, yet it remains, after nearly a century and a half—still gay, still charming.

Letters written for a practical purpose or to people whom you hardly know will naturally demand a different style from personal letters, whose chief end is to give pleasure. In the first kind of letter, clearness and accuracy are the chief essentials. Many people believe that a letter to be business-like must bristle with business terms—" Received your favour of the 16th inst." " Yours of the 21st to hand," etc., etc. Such jargon merely obscures what it wishes to make clear. The following letter from T. H. Huxley to Matthew Arnold might serve as a model for clearness and force, though it is of course not a business letter.

26 ABBEY PLACE,
July 8th.

DEAR ARNOLD,

Look at Bishop Wilson on the sin of covetousness and then inspect your umbrella stand. You will see there a beautiful brown smooth-handled umbrella which is not your property.

Think of what the excellent prelate would have advised, and bring it with you next time you come to the club.   The porter will take care of it for me.

Ever yours faithfully,
T. H. HUXLEY.

This example shows how a letter should be set out.   The first thing to write is the place from which, and the date at which it is written.   A date always has a certain value, even when the letter is quite recent : and this value goes on increasing with the years.   As to the place of writing, every letter—even those of the most intimate character—should bear at the top right-hand corner the address of the sender in sufficient fulness for postal purposes.   If the letter by any chance goes astray, the postal authorities can do nothing with it if it bears no trace of its origin ; and the case is no better if the address is some such vague term as Home : London.

The next thing is the address to the person to whom you are writing.   The most formal beginning is *Sir*.   All letters to Government officials should begin in this way, and should end *I have the honour to be, Sir, Your obedient Servant*.

The more usual form in business is the conventional *Dear Sir*.   This beginning implies a relation of friendly equality between the correspondents, but it does not imply that they are acquainted with or have ever even seen each other.   The ending for a letter of this kind corresponds to the beginning : *Yours faithfully*, *Yours truly*, *Yours sincerely*, rank in ascending order of friendliness.   The first is the most common of all, but the second is almost as colourless.   Into the third there creeps a shade of personal friendliness.

My dear Sir marks a certain amount of personal interest in your correspondent. It should not be used in a purely business letter, unless your correspondent is a personal friend as well as a business connection. The natural ending demanded by this beginning is *Yours very truly*, or *Yours most sincerely*. There are many people who dislike these adverbs *very* and *most* at the end of letters. With respect to grammar this dislike is justified : *truly, sincerely* and *faithfully* are not words that admit of comparison. If one is true, sincere, or faithful there is no more to be said. One is either sincere or one is not. The only justifiable qualification would be a time limit. *Yours sincerely on most occasions*, or *Yours at all times faithfully*. After admitting the literal inaccuracy of the forms, we may frankly recognise them as existing, and as useful to indicate certain degrees of friendliness.

The following beginnings of letters addressed to John Smith are arranged in ascending order of intimacy : *Dear Mr. Smith, My dear Mr. Smith, Dear Smith, Dear John*. People who regard themselves as authorities quarrel over the claims of *Dear Smith* and *My dear Smith* to the higher degree of intimacy. The difference between the two really seems to be that *My dear Smith* commits one to a somewhat friendlier relation with him than is implied in the shorter form. The same slight distinction holds between *Dear John* and *My dear John*. We use the Christian name only with relations or with those whom we have known in our childhood. It is safe to avoid this form in all the other cases of mere friendship.

The endings of letters begun on the model of

the John Smith series may end in *Yours truly, or sincerely, or very truly,* or *most sincerely.* As a rule *faithfully* is rather cold for this form. *Yours ever* is a conveniently brief and easy ending to a letter that begins *Dear Smith* or *Dear John.* As a matter of fact, both beginnings and endings in all except purely business letters depend to a great extent on the temperament of the writer. Every one is entitled to follow his own bent in private letters : but the rule in all cases of doubt is to use the colder form. *Dear Sir* and *Yours truly* commit one to nothing. *My dear Sir* and *Yours most sincerely* ought to mean a little more than the recognition of your correspondent as a civilised fellow-creature.

In business letters in which the name of our correspondent does not occur, it is necessary to write his name immediately before the *Dear Sir,* or else in the left-hand bottom corner of the page on which you finish the letter. It is usual and desirable to add his address. We must not depend upon the envelope to tell us to whom the letter was originally sent.

It is literally true that it takes at least two to write a letter. The person you write to has almost as much to do with your letter as you yourself have. If you examine two letters written by the same person describing the same circumstances to two different correspondents, you will find the letters as different as are the correspondents, and the better the letter-writer the more different will the two letters be. The first quality of a good letter-writer, indeed, is this very power of responding easily to the influence of the correspondent. A good letter is always written from the point of view of the person for whom it is meant. Naturally this does not mean that we must always accept the views of those to whom we write, but we must so express our views that they may fit in most easily with the mental habits of our correspondents. Even when we wish to make a man adopt our view, we must begin by looking at the matter from his standpoint.

That we all naturally do adopt the standpoint of our correspondent is proved by the prevalence in letters of a peculiar kind of technical error. We write for example : " I hope to come to you on the 27th at latest ". As a matter of strict accuracy we hope to *go,* not to *come.* But since we unconsciously adopt the correspondent's point of view we speak of coming.

Exercise 27

George Maidenhead, foreign correspondence clerk in a large London office, finds on his arrival at 13 Ingleborough Avenue, Wirencester, where he is to spend a fortnight's holiday, that he has lost the umbrella that his wealthy Aunt Matilda gave him as a birthday present. It is a silk umbrella, with a thin wooden shaft of a green colour : the handle is straight (*i.e.,* there is no hook or cross bar) and silver-mounted. He *thinks* he took it with him from his rooms in Montague Street, kept it beside him in the office all day, took it to Euston Road Station, put it in the rack in a third-class compartment in the 3 P.M. train for Bletchley, where he arrived at 4.58 P.M., and changed carriages for Wirencester, where he arrived at 6.11 P.M. Maidenhead has expectations from Aunt Matilda, who is to be a fellow-visitor with him at the Rushton's in Wirencester. He arrives on the 16th July, 1937. She is to arrive on the 18th. She is jealous about the respect paid to her presents. He must recover the umbrella before her arrival, and has already made fruitless inquiries about the lost umbrella at Wirencester Station.

Write such a letter as he might send to—

(*a*) The stationmaster at Bletchley, inquiring if the umbrella has been found, offering a reward of 10s., and the payment of all expenses of a search.

(*b*) To his landlady, Mrs. Hickson, to make sure that he has not left the umbrella in his rooms, and directing how to send the umbrella if found.

(*c*) To his fellow-clerk, Jerkyns, to inquire whether the umbrella has not been left in the office, and urging immediate despatch of umbrella if found.

(*d*) To his sister, Violet, living at home in the same town as Aunt Matilda. He encloses P.O.O. for 30s. to buy and send on to him an umbrella as like the aunt's present as possible. Violet has seen the original, and George assumes that it was bought at Akenside's, the local umbrella shop. Violet is not to buy the umbrella unless she receives a wire next day (*i.e.*, the 17th) with the order *buy* : this wire is to arrive before noon, else she is to understand that the lost umbrella has turned up.

LESSON XXVIII

THE ESSAY—HEADS

By an essay is usually understood an attempt to treat a subject in the way most suitable for a given occasion. There is often a didactic tone about the essay, its business seems to be to teach its readers. If we read an essay on Bimetallism or on Bivalves we expect to be instructed. Yet many of our best essayists are read merely for the charm of their style : we read them because we enjoy them, not because we learn from them. The amount of instruction we gather from reading Charles Lamb's " Dissertation upon Roast Pig " would never justify the time spent in reading that charming production. The word dissertation, here used in a whimsical sense, is generally applied to a serious and somewhat long essay. If a subject is discussed at great length the result should be called a treatise : but it is generally felt that *essay* is a more modest name. Accordingly we find some very important works known as essays, notably the most striking book on philosophy in the English Language— Locke's *Essay Concerning Human Understanding*. Though usually written in prose, an essay may take the form of verse, as in Pope's *Essay on Man*.

For our purpose an essay must be regarded as an attempt to express in a brief form our views upon any subject. It implies the selection of the proper matter, and the choice of the best way of expressing that matter. At first, therefore, it is well to write on subjects with which you are familiar. This will save you the excessive labour involved in doing two different things at the same time—discovering what to say and how to say it. The how is sufficient in itself to occupy all your attention.

Suppose the subject to be " My Favourite Book ", you are clearly assumed to know all about the book, yet you may find considerable difficulty in determining how to proceed. You may treat your favourite merely as an object, give a full description of its size, general appearance, type, paper, binding and so forth. You will find that you have material here for a complete little essay. Then you may deal with the question, Why is this book my favourite ? Here you will find yourself writing half about the book and half about yourself, and a complete little essay will result. Again you may examine the place of the book in English literature, and give a history of it ; or you may treat the matter of the book as subject for criticism ; or the style of the book may become your subject.

Each of these would make a complete essay, but very frequently parts may be taken from each and welded into a harmonious whole. It is here that the skill of arrangement is called into play. The essay must not be a thing of shreds and patches. It may treat only one aspect of a subject, and be complete so far as it goes ; but if it takes up two or three aspects, these must be so related to one another as to be seen to be parts of one whole.

Assuming that you are dealing with a subject about which you know something, and that you have selected the point of view from which you propose to treat it, you must set about preparing a few " heads " to keep you from mere rambling. It is indeed surprising how many ideas " come out of the ink-pot " when you sit down to write. You may think you have little to say on a subject, but somehow one thing suggests another till you find you have written quite a long essay. This method of following the suggestion of the moment is to be avoided. Some of our best writers no doubt write their pleasantest essays in this way, and when you have formed your style and acquired habits of logical arrangement you too may let yourself go, and follow the lead of association. But at your present stage you must guide your associations.

You should practise writing essays containing about as much matter as two pages of this book. For this kind of essay there should be at least three heads, each head representing a paragraph in the finished essay. Each head again should have sub-heads under it, and in some cases there may even be sub-sub-heads. You will understand this better by examining the following illustration.

Suppose the subject given is *The Style is the Man*, we might draw up some such notes as the following :—

I. In its widest sense this means that we are known by our manifestations.

> By their deeds shall ye know them.
> Manners makyth man.

II. Special meaning limited to a man's manner of writing.

F 165

A. Writing is expression of highest part of man's nature.

B. Style may be the man even though we cannot read the true man in it.

    (a) Compare Johnson's style and character.

    (b) Compare Rousseau's style and character.

III. Confusion between style and matter.

A. It does not follow that Sterne was kind because he wrote sympathetically. Thackeray the cynical writer was a kindlier man in reality than was Dickens the sentimentalist.

B. Style probably limited to the intellectual aspect of character.
The style is the head rather than the man.

While the beginner should always prepare heads for his essay, he should keep them private. The cupboard is the place for literary as well as for family skeletons. Your methodical student thinks otherwise. As soon as he gets the idea of the scheme of heads and sub-heads he is proud of it, and proceeds shamelessly to expose the scaffolding of his essay. He begins :—

First, let us consider it in its widest sense. . . .
Now let us consider it in its special sense, which may be divided under two main heads. . . .
Finally, let us consider the confusion between style and matter. . . .

Students are led to this display of the inner workings of their minds by the example of public speakers, notably clergymen. But the cases are not parallel. The audience or the congregation require much more help than the reader. He can take his own time, and can turn back at any moment to examine something that has gone before. The audience must take things as they come, and if anything is missed it is gone for ever. It is right, therefore, that the speaker should give them all the help possible by indicating beforehand the general line he is about to follow, and by mentioning anew each important head as he comes to it.

Certain essays too of a severe, argumentative type may have some of their sub-heads boldly stated. For example, the arguments for a given theory may be tabulated and numbered. But even here the whole skeleton need not be exposed : a rib or two will do quite well. With an ordinary essay the heads ought to be there for the seeking, but they should be decently covered up. The essay should read all the more smoothly because of the heads.

Exercise 28

Write a short pleasant essay on " Getting up on Cold Mornings ". (Do not be afraid to treat it from a personal angle.)

LESSON XXIX

THE ESSAY—BEGINNINGS AND ENDINGS

Take up a book of essays, preferably a book of essays selected from many different authors, and turn over the pages, noting carefully the first sentences of each essay. You will find it extremely interesting to observe how each begins, and a second rapid glance through the book will provide an equally interesting study of how each essay ends.

Some writers are fond of beginning with a striking sentence, and frequently call in the aid of somebody else. Augustine Birrell confesses that he likes " to leap-frog into his subject " over the back of a fellow-author, and if not too frequently used, this mode of opening an essay is very effective. Green, the historian, begins his examination of the character of King John with the words of a thirteenth-century writer : " Foul as it is, hell itself is defiled by the fouler presence of John ". Nothing could be more direct or more striking. Sometimes the quotation is indirect, and the point lies rather in the setting. Robert Louis Stevenson begins his essay on " Truth of Intercourse " : " Among sayings that have a currency in spite of being wholly false upon the face of them, for the sake of a half truth upon another subject which is accidentally combined with the error, one of the grossest and broadest conveys the monstrous proposition that it is easy to tell the truth and hard to tell a lie ". This is not so striking, but it arouses our interest by its contradiction of a popular saying. Stevenson is not here brief enough to claim an epigrammatic beginning : but the epigram, especially if it takes the form of a paradox, makes a very effective opening. Thus Charles Lamb begins his essay on " New Year's Eve " with the words : " Every man hath two birthdays ".

A plain, straightforward beginning is a definition of one's subject. Swift begins his essay on " Good Manners " : " Good manners is the art of making those people easy with whom we converse ". This is a literal definition, but sometimes a fantastic description of the subject takes the place of the more exact logical form. Charles Lamb thus introduces his essay on " Poor Relations " : " A poor relation is the most irrelevant thing in nature—a piece of impertinent correspondency—an odious approximation—a haunting conscience—a preposterous shadow lengthening in the noontide of our prosperity—an unwelcome remembrancer—a perpetually recurring mortification . . ." and so on with another score of whimsical equivalents.

A statement of the problem to be discussed makes an excellent start. Stevenson thus introduces his " Plea for Gas Lamps " : " Cities given, the problem was to light them ". But this style of opening in the hands of an ordinary writer is very liable to be dull. The interrogative beginning, as " Is Alpine climbing justifiable ? " is in itself good enough, but it has been so much abused by tired journalists that it had better be avoided.

The exclamatory beginning may be permitted in dealing with suitable subjects, but it must be rigidly kept to its own place. John Wilson may begin his essay on streams : " How delightful even to elders like us to feel Spring breathing once more over air and earth ! " But the ordinary prose writer will find it advisable to begin without the help of the exclamation mark. You must not here confound two totally different things. A beginning is not an introduction. No essay can do without a beginning, but most are all the better for lacking an introduction. If you examine all the beginnings now from the point of view of matter, you will find that in almost every case the first sentence tells us something that is of real importance in the essay. In other words, the best essayists begin at once, they do not require a paragraph to say that they are going to begin. An essay on female education was thus introduced by a student in an examination paper :—

" As soon as my eyes fell upon these words on my paper of questions, my heart misgave me. I know little about education, and nothing at all about female education, since my life-work will not run on these lines; but as the subject is prescribed I must do something, even if I have to adopt the method of the man who wrote an essay on Chinese hieroglyphics, by first of all reading all he could find about China and then all he could find about hieroglyphics, and finally combining the two kinds of knowledge thus acquired."

Clearly all this is irrelevant and must be struck out. It has nothing to do with female education, though it may have a great deal to do with covering a certain number of sheets at an examination.

Compare Sydney Smith's first sentences on the same subject : " A great deal has been said of the original difference of capacity between men and women; as if women were more quick, and men more judicious—as if women were more remarkable for delicacy of association, and men for stronger powers of attention. All this, we confess, appears to us very fanciful." Here female education is not even mentioned, and yet we feel that we are in the middle of the subject.

However the essay begins it must take an immediate grip of the reader. In order to catch the attention one need not be startling. Many of the essays by our best writers begin in the most unobtrusive way—perhaps the most common beginning of all is the simple impersonal formula *It is*—but they all get at once into their subject. Writers vary in the way they distribute interest throughout the essay. Some begin with minimum interest, go on to maximum interest, and end with medium interest. Others begin with maximum, fall gradually to minimum, and then gradually increase to maximum. When a difficult problem is being dealt with in which point after point is elucidated, there is a steady rise in interest from the beginning to the end. Interest begets interest in essays as well as in old-fashioned bank balances.

Whatever the general distribution of interest, there must be no fall *near* the end, though *at* the end a fall there must be, else the essay is not complete. The end of a good essay is coincident with the dissipation of interest. The interest ceases because the mind is satisfied.

The ending has the choice of most of the forms referred to as possible beginnings—a quotation, an epigram, a broad generalisation, a striking concrete example of some principle expounded in the essay. Yet the purpose of the end is quite different from that of the beginning. The purpose is not now to rouse and stimulate, but to satisfy. One essential characteristic of an ending is that it should be felt to be an ending. This does not mean that the essay should begin towards the end to wind itself up. The closing paragraph may not be recognised as the close of the essay, but the final sentence should leave no doubt on the matter. The ending of the estimate of King John of which we have already quoted the startling beginning is admirable : " The awful lesson of his life rests on the fact that it was no weak and indolent voluptuary, but the ablest and most ruthless of the Angevins who lost Normandy, became the vassal of the Pope, and perished in a struggle of despair against English freedom ". We feel that there is no more to be said.

" Truth of Intercourse " ends : " But the morality of the thing you will be glad to hear is excellent ; for it is only by trying to understand others that we can get our own hearts understood ; and in matters of human feeling the clement judge is the most successful pleader ". Here the wide general statement with its special application produces a feeling that the matter is settled, and we may attend to something else.

It would be mere affectation to pretend to expect anything more about New Year's Eve after Lamb has said, " And now another cup of the generous ! and a merry New Year, and many of them, to you all, my masters ! " His ending of " Poor Relations " is equally pointed.

" This was—a Poor Relation." This repetition of the title—a favourite trick at the end of amusing plays—must be sparingly used in essays.

Exercise 29

Make up a scheme of " heads " and sub-heads for essays on the following subjects—each essay to have at least three main heads.

(*a*) The Renaissance.
(*b*) The Exception Proves the Rule.

LESSON XXX

THE ESSAY—PREPARATION OF MATTER

You must now get some practice in preparing to write on subjects with which you are less familiar. Here you must read before you write. It is well to choose such a subject as may repay this preliminary reading and thinking. If you have no interest in natural history it would be a pity to read up all about insects in order to write an essay on the *Ravages of the Colorado Beetle*. Further, you should choose a subject that admits of complete preparation within a limited time. The preliminary reading for an essay on *The Elizabethan Literature*, or even for one on *The Elizabethan Dramatists* is a matter of several years of hard work. Many of the books on Shakespeare alone, embody the work of a lifetime. But take now a subject like *Shakespeare's Treatment of the Supernatural.* Here the range of preliminary reading is absolutely limited. It is true that if you wish to write an essay exhaustive enough to satisfy Shakespearean scholars you must read all that the critics—English, American and Continental—have said on this subject. But for a first-hand essay by a student all that need be read is Shakespeare himself.

It seems a disproportionate demand that all Shakespeare should be read in order to write an exercise. But if you have not yet read Shakespeare the sooner you begin the better, and if you have read him you will be all the better for looking over again the parts that deal with the supernatural. There is no better exercise in literature than to read over a known author to find his connection with a given aspect of his work.

If you have not read Shakespeare before, there is nothing for it but to read the whole of his plays. No other method will give you the right to treat the subject at all; for even when the supernatural is not prominently introduced it is frequently implied, and Shakespeare's treatment must be held to include indirect as well as direct use of his materials.

If you do not know Shakespeare and are afraid to undertake the whole of his works at once, the next best thing is to read over the *Dramatis Personæ* at the beginning of each of the plays. Your examination will direct you to those that make the most striking use of the supernatural. This will give *The Tempest, A Midsummer Night's Dream, Richard III., Macbeth, Hamlet.*

To these you had better add the first part of *Henry IV.*, the first and second parts of *Henry VI.* and *Julius Cæsar*. Having read these you will have a fair idea of Shakespeare's style, and a first-hand acquaintance with his methods of dealing with the supernatural. It may be convenient to keep separate his use of supernatural agents as *dramatis personæ* from his use of the supernatural as an element in human experience, and therefore an agent in the development and portrayal of character. His supernatural characters fall naturally into three classes : fairies, ghosts and witches.

We have now clearly two main heads : the direct use and the indirect; and in an essay by a student there can be no doubt that most attention should be given to the direct use. Since this essay should run to about ten or twelve pages of this book, it can stand a short introduction, if this introduction has some real connection with the subject.

The following set of heads gives a fair idea of a suitable way of selecting and grouping the matter for this essay. Examine the different heads carefully, treating each as a hint for further thought and investigation, and then write out an essay embodying the heads and extending to about a dozen pages of this book. When finished, this essay should be compared with that supplied at the end of Part II. This closing essay was written by a student, and represents the level to which you may be fairly expected to attain.

Introduction. " After God, Shakespeare created most." (Victor Hugo) : the two worlds of his creation.

Shakespeare's broad human sympathies are carried over into Cloudland.

Limitation of supernatural characters—gives reality.

Modern fairies lacking humanity are mere abstractions.

Direct use of supernatural.

Fairies.

Contrast of Puck and Ariel—as illustrating Shakespeare's idea of fairy nature.

Underlying meaning—prominent in *Tempest*, less so in *Midsummer Night's Dream*. Never obtruded.

Allowed to break down when to keep it up would injure the story.

Ghosts.

Command our belief more readily.

No underlying meaning—they do their duty and go.

Fail on ideal side—mere means to ends.

Witches.

Rank in interest intermediate between fairies and ghosts.

Rank highest in probability.

More scope for underlying meanings—*e.g.*, three tenses, three witches.

Motif of *Macbeth*—story not sacrificed to moral or theory.

Subordinate use of supernatural.

The supernatural as supplying an atmosphere.

The supernatural in expressing character.

Mere superstition.

SUGGESTIONS FOR FURTHER STUDY

Now that you have progressed thus far in the art of writing, you will profit by reading something of the theory of style. This can best be learnt from those who are accomplished writers themselves, for they discuss the writer's problems in the light of their own experience.

Herbert Spencer has an interesting essay on *The Philosophy of Style*. It is a good one to begin on, for it is short (only thirty-four pages), and very clearly set out. You may not agree with all his conclusions—indeed, it will be better if you do not, for then you will be forced to think the matter out for yourself. Sir Walter Raleigh, who was for a long time professor of English at Oxford, has left a very fine essay *On Style*, and he has some very good things to say in his notes *On Writing and Writers*. He is worth reading not only for what he says, but for his own brilliant style, and for his exact and scrupulous use of words. " Q ", who is a novelist as well as a professor, has written a book, *The Art of Writing*, which you will find delightful reading ; and, if you are interested in the theory of style, you will like the essays by the novelist, C. E. Montague, entitled *A Writer's Notes on his Trade*. In *The Craft of Fiction* Percy Lubbock discusses the technique of the novel, and illustrates the different methods of constructing a novel. Even though you do not wish to write a novel yourself, Mr. Lubbock's book will give you a keener interest in the novels you read. You are not likely to read all of these, immediately, one after another, but try at least to read Herbert

Spencer's essay and Q's lectures on the *Art of Writing*, and reserve the others for future study. You will find them interesting in themselves, as well as of practical value.

If you have little leisure for general reading, see that what you read is good. Your familiarity with good prose sets a standard for your own, and by steady reading you will keep that standard in mind. It is well to read as widely as possible, for in this way you will widen your vocabulary, as well as your interests and knowledge. Some people find it a good plan to have several books on hand at the same time, each one being of a different character. They will, for instance, be reading a novel, a biography and some more serious book on history, politics or art—all three more or less concurrently, according to their mood. If you find this method confusing, you should at any rate vary the kind of books you read. If you read any foreign language, you should keep up the habit of translating into English, not making a literal translation, but re-casting the material into good idiomatic prose. In this way you will gain readiness in the use of words, which is as important as learning new ones.

At this stage your style will be less easily influenced by reading authors with a highly individual style, whom you were discouraged from reading in the first chapter of this book. From Lamb you can learn very much about the technique of the essay, for in the *Essays of Elia* he has used all his art to produce an effect of ease and artlessness. Read them carefully, noticing the skilful way the style is adapted to the mood and the many changes of style within

the compass of a single essay. The essays of
Max Beerbohm and G. K. Chesterton will show you
how many unusual ways there are of treating a
seemingly ordinary subject—you might take
Max Beerbohm's essay " An Infamous Brigade ",
and Chesterton's " What I found in my Pocket "
as especially good examples. Their dazzling
style is, of course, beyond imitation.

Robert Louis Stevenson tells how he worked
out his own style by deliberately imitating other
people's, writing passages now in the style of one,
now of another. This is easier than it sounds,
for after reading any author for a little time, you
will find that, when you write, you unconsciously
adopt some of the characteristics of his style.
It is a more difficult matter to re-write a passage
from one author in the style of another—to
reproduce a passage from Ruskin, for example,
in the style of Carlyle, or a passage from Johnson
in the style of Charles Lamb. It is amusing to
attempt this, but extremely difficult to do it
well, since it is rarely that form and matter can
be easily separated. You will find it easier to
practise the first kind of imitation, and you
should practise it regularly. After you have
read a book by any writer with a fairly pronounced style, set yourself to write a short
passage on a subject he might himself have
chosen, imitating as far as possible his customary
rhythm and balance, and using a vocabulary
similar to his own. If, for instance, you have
been reading Lamb's essay, " Mrs. Battle's
Opinions on Whist ", then try to write a short
character sketch of someone you know, modelling
your style on the crisp, incisive style of the
first three paragraphs of that essay. This

practice in imitation will give your style greater flexibility and wider range. The charm of a good style is that it is never monotonous, but offers a continual variety.

Journal-keeping should by now have become a steady habit, and you will have gained from it, not only greater fluency, but greater power of observation. As you gain power to express what you see, so you see more to express. But you must practise other more formal modes of writing, essays, narrative, exact description. If you wish to write fiction, you will be best at first to confine yourself to fact. Fiction is, after all, only the imaginative handling of facts. The imagination creates nothing of itself, but merely transmutes experience, and you will not be able to write well on anything that is outside your experience. If you write stories, let them be about people such as you know yourself, and set them against a familiar background. If you go beyond it, you will not only make mistakes in detail, but you will create characters who are not real people, but dummies in fancy dress.

It is wiser not to confine yourself to one form of composition, or to one style of writing. If you are fond of a poetical diction, a course of writing on exact subjects with plenty of statistics is a good counterpoise. If you are given to bald statements of fact, you should practise on subjects involving a certain amount of feeling. If you tend naturally to abstractions, practise yourself in dealing with the concrete. You aim is to get a grip of language, to master it, to make it obey your will. If you write only in the way you like, and on subjects you are fond of, your grip of language is limited, you become lopsided and can treat a subject only in one way. You become the subject of language, not the master.

A very valuable exercise is to read articles by different authors on the same subject. Opportunities for this comparative method are to be found almost every month in the more serious periodicals. There is usually some subject of general interest treated in two or three of these, and it is very instructive to compare the points of view, the arrangement of matter, the tone, the vocabulary. After reading such articles critically for a month or two you cannot do better than try the experiment of writing an article yourself on some subject that you find in one or two of them, and then compare your work with the printed matter.

One great advantage of the study of articles by competent writers in the more serious periodicals is the training it gives in the perception of the proportions of the various parts of a subject. An inexperienced writer goes wrong more frequently in proportion than in anything else. To treat a wide subject within a narrow compass and maintain the relative importance of the different parts is the mark of an accomplished essayist. An excellent exercise is to make a skeleton outline, such as we used on page 165, to correspond to an article we are examining. You will be surprised to find how interesting this process of analysis becomes when intelligently practised. Many articles that read well, and seem all right on a general view, will be found to fail in proportion and arrangement when the test is applied of reducing them to their skeletons. Here, as elsewhere, we must be on our guard against pedantry. If we are dealing with a light article whose purpose is to produce a certain more or less pleasurable impression, we must not exact just proportion as measured by arithmetical standards. The criterion of success is the impression produced. But in a seriously reasoned-out article proportion must be observed or the reasoning itself must suffer. So important is this matter of proportion that a weekly analysis of a serious article, solely from this point of view, is not too much.

Set aside a definite period for work, and work systematically, not despairing though your progress seem slow. A good style is the reward of long practice. It is not a natural gift bestowed at birth by some good fairy, but is only to be gained by hard work and an infinity of pains. Yet it can be gained if we will spare the time and trouble. Everyone has the power to write well, though to write very well be the prerogative of few.

PART II

KEY TO EXERCISES

Exercise 1

(a) 1. *Derogatory*. The word *derogative* does not exist. 2. *Observance*. *Observation* means looking at something so as to learn more about it. 3. *Profitable*, or *lucrative*. *Payable* implies that something must *be* paid. 4. *Dissension*. *Dissent* lays stress on difference of opinion : *dissension* lays stress on the resulting discord. 5. *Contemptuously*. *Contemptible* means worthy of contempt, *contemptuous* full of contempt for somebody or something. 6. *Healthful*. 7. *Die*. 8. *Spoiling*. *Spoliation* has become equivalent to plundering. 9. The girl was *homesick*. *Nostalgia* is a big word meaning homesickness. 10. *Imply*. We usually infer *from*, and imply *by*. 11. *Break*. 12. *Luxuriant*. *Luxurious* means given to luxury : *luxuriant* means abundant. 13. *Acceptance*. *Acceptation* has become narrowed down so that it applies to words only. 14. *Act*. Action is not usually applied to a single uncomplicated deed. 15. *Discovery*. We discover what was there already though unknown, for example planets or old manuscripts. We invent something that did not before exist, for example a steam engine. The compound called chloroform was discovered. Its application to surgery may be called an invention. 16. *Human*.

(b) 1. Shadowy, translucent, limpid, sparkling, glassy, glittering, dappled, tranquil, placid, rippling, low-lapping. 2. Shining, mysterious, iron-grey, opaque, oily, sluggish, turgid, un-hurrying, majestic, noiseless, slow-sliding. (Many of these adjectives might serve to describe both.)

Exercise 2

(a) 1. *Interesting*. *Entertaining* originally meant " *holding the attention* " : now it is nearly equivalent to *amusing*. 2. *Wistfully*. This is almost the same as *wishfully*, but is acquiring a connection with things that are unattainable. 3. *Fraud* refers more to the action done, *guile* to the character of the persons acting. 4. *Adjoining* is inaccurate since the islands are not joined, *contiguous* is inapplicable since they do not touch, *neighbouring* is, perhaps, the nearest equivalent. 5. *Determined* implies indifference to the opinions of others, *resolute* indifference to the consequences of our actions. 6. *Delinquents* refers more to sins of omission, *offenders* to sins of commission. 7. *Funeral* is felt to be much less imposing. 8. *Obliged* is usually used of a slight service : we can be *indebted* to things, but obliged only to persons. 9. *Survives* implies *going on living* after something else has gone : *outlives* merely means that we live long enough to see the end of the other thing. 10. *Marriage* refers to the state, *wedding* to the initial ceremony. 11. *Balls*. All globes are balls, but all balls are not globes. 12. *Disgrace* is not quite so bad as *reproach*. 13. *Encroaches* includes *intrenchment* as well as other forms of pushing our way where we have no business. 14. *Detest* applies more to our intellect, *abhor* more to our feelings. 15. *Screamed* is not quite so shrill as *shrieked*, but it may last longer. 16. *Readable* rather implies worth reading, while *legible* refers to the mechanical difficulty of reading manuscript or type.

(*b*) 1. Impassive, immobile, monumental, majestic, wooden, phlegmatic, dignified, solemn, courteous, good-humoured, patient, officious, efficient. 2. Fervent, passionate, eager, intense, scornful, ironic, patient, exasperated, hectoring, shrill, factious, earnest, pathetic, ridiculous.

Exercise 3

1. The Opposition must bestir themselves if they wish to gain anything at the approaching election. 2. The judges had a military escort to their hotel. 3. Omit " religious ". 4. Mr. Parkins of this city died last night. 5. It is rumoured that jealousy was the cause of the tragedy that occurred. . . . 6. The distinguished party had a cold supper at midnight. 7. The authorities were shocked when they learned how wildly the newcomers had behaved in the town. 8. The Government was utterly rotten. [Garboard-streak is the name of the plank next the keel—but the general reader cannot be expected to know that.] 9. Open-air meals ——. 10. The Countess is shortly to give birth to a child. 11. Do not work at this exercise till midnight. 12. I drink cocoa regularly every night. 13. In science Einstein is pre-eminent. 14. He suffers from a strong sense of his own inferiority. 15. She declared she loved birds. 16. Uncorrupted conduct is very desirable. 17. A really fashionable child

requires an engagement book in which to record her many social activities. 18. I am astounded (amazed, astonished, confounded, etc.) by the impertinence of the honourable member who has just spoken. (*Honourable member*, as a term of etiquette in the House of Commons, must not be changed.) 19. Now is the fitting moment for the restoration of the monarchy. 20. His book is worth reading.

Exercise 4

(*a*) 1. ―― his spirit never wavered. 2. It was bitter to fail ―― 3. ―― he entered the forbidden territory. 4. It was in your power ―― 5. The modern schoolmaster is expected ―― 6. ―― William proceeded to the Hague. 7. ―― the bubble increased for a time, but ultimately burst. 8. The success of the newspaper was not secured ―― 9. ―― set out for London. 10. It is mortifying ――

(*b*) (i) The cuckoo flies early to the south, leaving her young in another bird's nest. (ii) The town clock marks each hour with a noisy chime. (iii) The silver gleamed in the faint light of the candles.

Exercise 5

The important part of the sentence is, *we came to our journey's end*, and the position of this part really determines the character of the whole sentence. As the sentence stands in Part I. this important part comes first. Herbert

Spencer in his *Philosophy of Style* would put part of it in the middle and the rest at the end :—

(*a*) At last, with no small difficulty, and after much fatigue, we came, through deep roads and bad weather, to our journey's end.

Dr. Whately places the *came* nearer the end :—

(*b*) At last, after much fatigue, through deep roads and bad weather, we came, with no small difficulty, to our journey's end.

The important part may be thrown to the very end :—

(*c*) At last, with no small difficulty, after much fatigue, through deep roads, and bad weather, we came to our journey's end.

(*d*) . . . to our journey's end we came.

It is clear that by rearranging the various phrases we may produce a very great number of variations on the original. Thus we might begin :—

1. At last we came . . . 2. At last after much . . . 3. At last through deep . . . 4. At last through bad weather . . . 5. At last to our journey's end . . . we came.

So we might begin with, *After much fatigue* . . . and ring the same changes, and so with each of the phrases.

(*b*) We started out along the edge of a field. The barley was still grey-green. Then the path twisted through a little coppice. We could hear the churring of wood-pigeons. A rabbit ran across the path a few yards ahead. By the far gate a game-keeper had nailed a dead stoat and a jay to a branch. We supposed it was by way of warning. We stopped for tea at a farm-house.

There were small black pigs scampering about the yard. The farmer's wife gave us eggs and honey for tea. She charged us only a shilling each. We returned to the station by road.

Exercise 6

(a) 1. Is this English straightforwardness? 2. Where is a braver man to be found? 3. Who can doubt any longer about the matter? 4. Is there a scrap of evidence against him? [The answer is clearly, *No*. But if the question were : Is there any evidence against him? it would have to be treated as a mere question, and the answer would depend on circumstances. It is the word *scrap* that makes the difference.] 5. Am I a dog that I should do this thing?

(b) 1. What a very ugly mouth he has! [Or simply, What an ugly mouth he has! For the exclamatory form more than makes up for the loss of the *very*.] 2. How I dislike babies! 3. How wonderful are the ways of God! 4. What plunder! [Neither *plenty* nor *here* are required. They are really included in the two words of the exclamation.]

(c) I woke late. The room was very light. The ceiling had an unaccustomed whiteness. Footsteps outside sounded soft, muffled. On roof and chimney stack, street and garden, snow lay thick. The postman, padding from house to house, left diagonal tracks to and fro across the road. The lawn was patterned with sparrows' foot-prints. Snow began to fall again, softly, softly—white goose-feathers fluttering down.

Opening the window, I picked a snow-flake from the sill. It glittered a moment on my finger-tip, a bright filigree flower. Then it was gone. Faster came the snow, in a swirl and a flurry, out of a chalk-white sky. It twisted and danced in the air. I drew the bedclothes closer. Soon, men would put down salt to melt it. They would sweep it from the streets. But in the country it would lie outspread over field and farm and haystack. The air would be still, and muffled every sound. Under its white counterpane the earth would sleep.

Exercise 7

(a) 1. Principal verb : *is*.

There's a story
|
that the river's angry
|
when the mill changes hands.

2. Principal verb : *have*.

Nevertheless, we have reason to be thankful that the thing, well or ill, is over.

3. Principal verbs : *love, let.* The clauses are independent and of equal importance. 4. Principal verb : *could give.* The sentence, in spite of its length and apparent intricacy, is Simple.

(b) We started out along the edge of a field where the barley was still grey-green. The path twisted through a little coppice where we could hear wood-pigeons churring, and saw a

189

rabbit run across a few yards ahead. By the far gate a game-keeper had nailed a dead stoat and jay to a branch—by way of warning, we supposed. We stopped for tea at a farm-house where there were small black pigs scampering about the yard. The farmer's wife gave us eggs and honey for tea, and charged us only a shilling each. We returned to the station by the road.

Exercise 8

(a) 1. —— I never had a patron before. 2. —— impertinent. 3. —— offered a sacrifice to God. 4. —— presented an epitome of country abundance. 5. —— God disposes. 6. The manuscript was lost and —— 7. The prince himself interceded for the captives —— 8. The prince is merciful —— 9. —— followed his work amain. 10. —— threw an appealing look at Hepzibah. 11. The rumour was false; —— 12. —— he does not love her.

(b) When I woke at last, the room was very light; the ceiling had an unaccustomed whiteness, and footsteps outside sounded soft and muffled. I looked out of the window, and saw that on roof and chimney stack, street and garden, snow lay thick. The postman, padding from house to house, left diagonal tracks to and fro across the road; a sparrow's foot-prints patterned the velvet lawn. Snow began to fall again, softly, softly—white goose-feathers fluttering down. Opening the window, I picked one from the sill: it glittered a moment on my finger-tip, a bright filigree flower, and then was gone. Faster came the snow, in a swirl and a flurry, out of a chalk-white sky. It twisted and danced in the air. Soon men would put down salt to melt it, and would sweep it away; but in the country it would lie outspread over field and farm and haystack; the air would be still, and muffled every sound, and under its white counterpane the earth would sleep.

Exercise 9

1. (a) The man that had a widowed mother was exempted from military service. (b) The man, who had a widowed mother, was exempted from military service. 2. (a) The ship that Jackson & Co. built was wrecked. (b) The ship, which Jackson & Co. built, was wrecked : or, The ship was wrecked which Jackson & Co. built. 3. (a) The little lamb that Mary had went with her to school. (b) Mary had a little lamb which went with her to school. 4. (a) The novelist that is conceited and has few friends is despised : or, The novelist that is conceited has few friends and is despised. (b) The novelist, who is conceited and has few friends, is despised.

(b) Sir William used to show with pride a silver casket which he had received from an Indian prince. He had been able to accommodate him in a small matter which had arisen out of some diplomatic entanglements. These necessarily arise in a country whose rulers are kept at peace only by fear of the force which the government can bring to bear upon those who transgress the limits marked out for them.

(*Princes* can be omitted since it clearly refers to the *rulers* just mentioned. Such a sentence cannot be satisfactorily re-modelled, since its bad construction results from the looseness of the thought, and the attempt to group together ideas that are not closely related to each other.)

Exercise 10

(*a*) 1. Periodic: Edward the Black Prince reverenced the age, the station and the misfortunes of your king when he made him his prisoner; attending him, serving him, consoling him like a son. 2. Loose: If the knight had not called him to his side, complaining that the length and roughness of the roads had shaken his saddle so as to make it uneven and uneasy, the servant would, as became him, have kept behind his master. 3. Periodic: Strewing flowers before the funerals, and planting them at the graves of departed friends, are among the beautiful and simple-hearted customs of rural life which still linger in some parts of England. 4. Loose: When it is excited by the bounty and familiarity of their elders there is something genuine and affectionate in the gaiety of the young. 5. Loose: That the Aristotelians erected their castles upon a basis far less reliable than air is the simple truth. 6. Periodic: We must leave out of sight altogether such nothings as the speed of a cannon ball or of sound, when we attempt to appreciate this interval by the aid of any considerations of velocity, as we did in endeavouring to estimate the distance of the moon. 7. Periodic : They have a spirit indeed, they that pretend to have the Spirit and so turn away from the straight rule of the Holy Scriptures; but it is a fanatical spirit, the spirit of delusion and giddness. 8. Periodic : I am led to imagine that one of Ponto's black Hampshires had been sacrificed a short time before my visit, for the dinner was composed of pig's head mock-turtle soup, of pig's fry and roast ribs of pork.

(b) I love the city for the people in it : the endless ebb and flow of the crowd; the chance encounters, overheard conversations; the friendly bus conductors, the large solemn policeman; the whole gay, ridiculous, ever diverting cavalcade of my fellow-men.

To feel turf beneath my feet instead of dead pavement; clean wind in my face instead of dusty air; to know the changing beauty of trees instead of the monotonous sameness of houses—for this I would give all the luxury of Mayfair in exchange for a cottage in the country.

Exercise II

(a) It ought to be presumed that a respectable and honourable publisher will wind up his affairs respectably and honourably, however suddenly he may retire from business.

(b) Turning to Friday I said, " Now, Friday, do as I bid thee "; and when he said he would, I said, " Then, Friday, do exactly as you see me do—fail in nothing ". Note that this change is not for the better. The short sentences, as is explained in the text, are more effective.

(c) A very interesting case is now being treated at St. ——'s Hospital. The patient, the child of poor parents, had stolen from his sister a necklace of large wooden beads. In playing with them, he cut the string and swallowed a bead. Finding it extremely pleasant, he returned next day and swallowed two beads. On the day after he swallowed three, and in this way he went on, until by the end of the week he had swallowed the whole necklace—twenty-five beads in all. His sister was deeply grieved at the loss of her necklace and searched everywhere for it in vain. A few days afterwards, when the family were at dinner, and the child, not being hungry, was playing about the room, a loud rattling was suddenly heard like the sound of a small hailstorm. The father told the child to be quiet, but after a little, the noise broke out again, louder than ever. In annoyance, and by way of punishment, he shook the child. A tremendous rattling ensued. He thereupon declared with an oath that he must have croup in the wrong place, but the child, beginning to cry, confessed he had swallowed the necklace. The father promptly caught him up and carried him to the hospital, the beads in the boy's stomach rattling all the way, so that, as they went by, people looked everywhere to see whence the unusual sound came. He is still in the hospital, and makes so much noise when he walks about that is necessary to muffle him in a watchman's coat for fear he should wake the patients.

Exercise 12

(*a*) Second paragraph begins: Sarah Battle was none of that breed; third paragraph begins: I never in my life; fourth paragraph begins: Pope was her favourite.

(*b*) The fruiterer's shop is easily the gayest in the street. Behind its plate-glass windows rises a hillside of oranges and apples; bananas are festooned above, and the grapes hang in heavy clusters ravishing the eye. What colour is here! Red-gold oranges, and the paler gold of lemons; tangerines in silver jackets, rosy Jonathon apples polished till they wink with brightness; soberer colours, too, in the freckled pears and pale field mushrooms—someone rose early in the grey morning to gather those! Most of the fruit has been brought from afar: oranges from Brazil and Africa and Spain, gathered months ago under the warm sun; lemons from Italy; little spotted bananas from the Canaries, and the big yellow ones from Jamaica; prickly South African pineapples, and stranger fruit besides, grenadillas, passion-fruit, persimmons—names out of romance. The seasons are turned topsy-turvy; all the fruits of summer are here in the November dusk. Only the English fruit keeps due season— Bramley's Seedlings, William pears, Cox's Orange Pippins—these shone on orchard trees not many weeks ago. With the brown beech leaves there on the shelf, and the tawny curled chrysanthemums, they are the last reminders of the autumn that is over.

Exercise 13

(a) 1. A man going to sea, his wife desires the prayers of the congregation. 2. The woman that deliberates is lost.

3. Ask where's the north? At York, 'tis on the Tweed;

In Scotland at the Orcades; and there

At Greenland, Zembla, or the Lord knows where.

4. At length Mary died: Elizabeth succeeded; and Cecil rose at once to greatness. 5. "And what did your uncle say to that?" asked the judge. "He said, 'You must never breathe a word of this to a living soul'", was the reply. 6. I go to a convention of philanthropists. Do what I can, I cannot keep my eyes off the clock. But if there should appear in the company some gentle soul who knows little of persons or parties, of Carolina or Cuba, but who announces a law that disposes these particulars, and so certifies me of the equity which checkmates every false player, bankrupts every self-seeker, and apprises me of my independence on any conditions of country, or time, or human body, that man liberates me; I forget the clock; I pass out of the sore relation to persons; I am healed of my hurts; I am made immortal by apprehending my possession of incorruptible goods. 7. If he was an inhumane old gentleman (and I am afraid it is a fact that he was inhumane), he was also perfectly intrepid. 8. He promised to go down first; and boldly he did so; for William, give him his due, had the heart of a lion.

9. " I'm no leech," said Adam. " Let me go."

"No—not yet. I will convict thee of ignorance. Thou dost not even know where the liver is placed."

" I do," answered Adam shortly ; " but what then ? "

" Thou dost—I deny it. Here is a pin ; stick it into this wax, man,[1] where thou sayest the liver lies in the human frame."

Adam unsuspiciously obeyed.

10. " You and I, Master Worthy, have worked hard many years, and think it very well to have scraped a trifle of money together ; you a few hundreds, I suppose, and I a few thousands."

(b) There was a table set out under a tree in front of the house, and the March Hare and the Hatter were having tea at it : a dormouse was sitting between them, fast asleep, and the other two were using it as a cushion, resting their elbows on it, and talking over its head. " Very uncomfortable for the dormouse," thought Alice ; " only, as it's fast asleep, I suppose it doesn't mind."

The table was a large one, but the three were all crowded together at one corner of it. " No room ! No room ! " they cried out when they saw Alice coming. " There's plenty of room ! " said Alice indignantly, and she sat down in a large armchair at one end of the table.

" Have some wine," the March Hare said in an encouraging tone.

Alice looked all round the table, but there

[1] *Man* is here nominative of address : *wax-man* would make equally good sense, though this is not what Lord Lytton meant.

was nothing on it but tea. "I don't see any wine," she remarked.

"There isn't any," said the March Hare.

"Then it wasn't very civil of you to offer it," said Alice angrily.

"It wasn't very civil of you to sit down without being invited," said the March Hare.

"I didn't know it was your table," said Alice; "it's laid for a great many more than three."

"Your hair wants cutting," said the Hatter. He had been looking at Alice for some time with great curiosity, and this was his first speech.

"You should learn not to make personal remarks," Alice said with some severity; "it's very rude."

The Hatter opened his eyes very wide on hearing this; but all he said was "Why is a raven like a writing desk?"

"Come, we shall have some fun now!" thought Alice. "I'm glad they've begun asking riddles—I believe I can guess that," she added aloud.

"Do you mean you think you can find out the answer to it?" said the March Hare.

"Exactly so," said Alice.

"Then you should say what you mean," the March Hare went on.

"I do," Alice hastily replied; "at least—at least I mean what I say—that's the same thing, you know."

(*Alice in Wonderland* : Lewis Carroll.)

Exercise 14

1. Babies rolled and tumbled about. (We have no right to add *in the grass*, since that refers to the fruit.) The metaphor is a pleasant one, and might be kept on that account, even if it is not very necessary. 2. Be silent. (Close your mouth is meant, but the size of the mouth is supposed to be so great that closing it is like closing the whole head.) The metaphor is much more effective. 3. When lovers are together they pay no attention to time. Metaphor is better, because shorter and neater. 4. The ashes of Mr. Foster's note curled up. The metaphor gives a much wider meaning here, for it suggests that the contents of the note were sour also. 5. He had failed in literature; he now turned to law. Literal form perhaps better, for the personification has been rather often used. 6. That shop, which was dark and smelt of Bibles, attracted all boys. Literal form better. It is difficult to think of the smell of the shop and then to imagine it as a loadstone. 7. Habit can be changed only by gentle means persistently applied. Metaphor more effective. 8. The very wood seems as if it sympathised with us in our troubles. This is clearly an emotional passage, and the personification is best suited to it. 9. Plenty of men are willing to abase themselves before those who will supply the good things of life. A very awkward metaphor in which eating truffles and licking blacking seem intended as equivalents. 10. Mrs. Agar ate very little. Metaphor so common as to be almost literal. 11. The lid of the

kettle cluttered noisily. The simile is unnecessary and tiresomely facetious. 12. An Ogilvie's sword could not pierce so deep as that. Metaphor suited to the somewhat elevated tone of the sentence. 13. His evil soul went shrieking down to its place. An effective simile in its context. 14. "No," said his daughter, preparing to combat him with tears. A very awkward metaphor. 15. With these words he withdrew, leaving his furious companion to pace the deck. A very awkward metaphor.

(b) The rocket rose and broke, *flowering* in sudden brightness. It fell *like a silver fountain* out of the black sky.

She *rode* the waves proudly. Then a wind sprang up, and she moved away down the strait *like a great white bird*.

The *greedy* water lapped closer. It advanced slowly, yet perceptibly, *like a stealthy ravenous beast*.

Exercise 15

1. Antithesis : This is a mild epigram, which is literal enough as it stands. 2. Hyperbole : another epigram. 3. Irony : The Duke of Wellington did not write good French. 4. Hyperbole : Some German words are extremely long. 5. Antithesis [also simile]. 6. Epigram. 7. Hyperbole : The hills in the south of Scotland are extremely bare. 8. Epigram. 9. Epigrammatic irony. 10. Metaphor : The people of Paris go mad. 11. Antithesis : All the advantages that age brings cannot equal the advantages which youth possesses. 12. Ironical

epigram : And the verse is very bad.   13. Antithetical epigram : Since we still love those we
lose, can we be said to have altogether lost them?
14. Antithesis and antithetical simile.   15. Euphemism : The Prime Minister was dismissed.

Exercise 16

(a) " I more than half guessed that there
might be some hanky-panky of this sort, and I
have therefore taken such steps as will prevent
me from being left out in the cold. I propose to
deal with this affair as I deal with matters of
politics or of organisation, that is, I shall use
plain language and speak out my mind like a
man. If a man or a woman behaves straight
to me I behave straight to them ; if they behave
crooked, I behave crooked. That's me all the
world over. Further if I were here and now to
undertake to write my own epitaph, I would simply
take a pen, dip it in the ink, seat myself at the
table, and write these words : ' He was as open
as the day '."

(b) " Fame is dear to the heart of every man.
Poetic fame is dear to the heart of my friend
Snodgrass ; the fame of conquest is equally
dear to my friend Tupman ; and the desire of
earning fame in the sports of the field, the air,
and the water is uppermost in the breast of my
friend Winkle. I will not deny that I am
influenced by human passions and human feelings
(cheers), possibly by human weaknesses (loud
cries of ' No '), but this I will say, that if ever the
fire of self-importance breaks out in my bosom

the desire to benefit the human race in preference
effectually quenches it. The praise of mankind
is my Swing; philanthropy is my insurance
office. (Vehement cheering.) I felt some pride
—I acknowledge it freely, and let my enemies
make the most of it—I felt some pride when I
presented my Tittlebatian Theory to the world;
it may be celebrated or it may not. (A cry of 'It is'
and great cheering.) I will take the assertion of
the[1] honourable Pickwickian whose voice I have
just heard—it is celebrated; but if the fame of that
treatise were to extend to the farthest confines
of the known world, the pride with which I
should reflect on the authorship of that production would be as nothing compared with the
pride with which I look around me on this, the
the proudest moment of my existence. (Cheers.)
I am a humble individual. ('No, no.') Still I
cannot but feel that you have selected me for a
service of great honour, and of some danger.
Travelling is in a troubled state, and the minds
of coachmen are unsettled. Look abroad and
contemplate the scenes which are enacting
around you. Stage coaches are upsetting in
all directions, horses are bolting, boats are
overturning, and boilers are bursting. (Cheers—
A voice, 'No'.) No! (Cheers.) Let the[1]
honourable Pickwickian who cried 'No' so
loudly come forward and deny it if he can.
(Cheers.) Who was it that cried 'No'? (Enthusiastic cheering.) Was it some vain and
disappointed man —I will not say haberdasher—
(loud cheers)—who jealous of the praise which

---

[1] In both these cases we might retain *that*, but since the
Pickwickian in each case is clearly pointed out by the
relative clause the definite article is sufficient.

has been—perhaps undeservedly—bestowed on my researches and smarting under the censure which has been heaped upon his own feeble attempts at rivalry, now takes this vile and calumnious mode of——"

Mr. BLOTTON (of Aldgate) rose to order. "Does the honourable Pickwickian allude to me?" (Cries of "Order", "Chair", "Yes", "No", "Go on", "Leave off", etc.)

Mr. PICKWICK. "I will not put up to be put down by clamour. I *did* allude to the honourable gentleman." (Great excitement.)

Mr. BLOTTON. "I shall only say then that I repel the honourable gentleman's false and scurrilous accusation with profound contempt. (Great cheering.) The honourable gentleman is a humbug."

(*c*) The atrocious crime of being a young man, which the honourable gentleman had, with such spirit and decency, charged upon him, he would neither attempt to palliate nor deny; but content himself with wishing that he might be one of those whose follies might cease with their youth, and not of those who continued ignorant in spite of age and experience.

Whether youth could be attributed to any man as a reproach he would not assume the province of determining; but surely age might justly become contemptible, if the opportunities which it brought had passed away without improvement, and vice appeared to prevail when the passions had subsided. The wretch who, after having seen the consequences of a thousand errors, continued still to blunder, and in whom age had only added obstinacy to stupidity, was surely the object either of abhorrence or contempt; and deserved not that his grey head should secure him from insults. Much more was to to be abhorred, who, as he had advanced in age, had receded from virtue, and become more wicked with less temptation; who prostituted himself for money which he could not enjoy, and spent the remains of his life in the ruin of his country.

(*d*) He could not, he assured their lordships, he would not, join in congratulation on misfortune and disgrace. That was a perilous and tremendous moment. It was not a time for adulation : the smoothness of flattery could not save them in that rugged and awful crisis. It was then necessary to instruct the throne in the language of truth. They must if possible dispel the delusion and darkness which enveloped it; and display, in its full danger and genuine colours, the ruin which was brought to their doors. Could ministers still presume to expect support in their infatuation? Could Parliament be so dead to its dignity and duty, as to give its support to measures thus obtruded and forced upon it? Measures, he assured their lordships, which had reduced that late flourishing empire to scorn and contempt! " But yesterday, and Britain might have stood against the world : now none so poor as do her reverence ! " That people whom they had at first despised as rebels, but whom they had now acknowledged as enemies, were abetted against them, supplied with every military store, had their interests consulted, and their (the Americans') ambassadors entertained by their (Britain's) inveterate enemy ; and ministers did not—and dared not—interpose with dignity or effect. The desperate state of their army

abroad was in part known. No man more
highly esteemed and honoured the British troops
than he did; he knew their virtues and their
valour; he knew they could achieve anything
but impossibilities; and he knew that the
conquest of British America was an impossibility.
They could not, he told their lordships, they could
not conquer America. What was their present
situation there? They did not know the worst;
but they knew that in three campaigns they had
done nothing and had suffered much. They
might swell every expense, accumulate every
assistance, and extend their traffic to the
shambles of every German despot: their
attempts would be for ever vain and impotent.

Exercise 17

Mrs. Dash-Blank has always found Susan
Liskens careful, honest and willing. Susan has
been in Mrs. Dash-Blank's service only nine
months, but she came with a four years' character
and has done nothing to forfeit it. Susan of her
own accord leaves Mrs. Dash-Blank.

Mr. Brown presents his compliments to Mr.
Johnson, and will be much obliged if Mr. Johnson will keep his dog on his own side of the
wall during the day, and on the side of the
house remote from Mr. Brown during the night
as neither Mr. Brown nor Mrs. Brown gets any
sleep while the dog occupies his present position.

If advertiser R. S., 4,309, will call on Mrs.
Spross at 47 Arlington Villas he will find a suite
of rooms that fulfills all the conditions he

H   205

specifies. Mrs. Spross can assure him that nothing will be wanting on her part to make him comfortable. She does her own washing, so the advertiser may rely upon having his linen well attended to.

Exercise 18

1. (a) For do I now persuade God or do I persuade men? (b) For do I now persuade God or do men persuade Him? 2. (a) We know little of his hearers as individuals. (b) We as individuals know little of his hearers. 3. (a) I shall read your verses at once. (b) I shall not waste time reading your verses. 4. (a) Drink to me with your eyes only. (b) Drink to me alone with your eyes. 5. (a) You cannot pass from that place where by His decree you are fixed. (b) By His decree you cannot pass from the place where you are fixed. 6. (a) . . . is a poor thing, a small portrait of, etc. (b) . . . who was sister of Rossetti and a poor thing. 7. (a) . . . character not the profession makes the man. (b) . . . makes the man but does not make the profession. 8. (a) That is either a man's voice or a woman's. (b) If that is not a man, it is the voice of a woman. 9. (a) For sale a fine bulldog which is fond of children and is not dainty about its food. (b) . . . eats anything, particularly children. 10. (a) The timid creatures . . . (b) The terrible creatures . . .

Exercise 19

(*a*) The Honourable Mrs. Jamieson, who has just left me, told me in the course of conversation that she had received a call yesterday from her husband's former friend, Lord Mauleverer. You will not easily guess what brought his lordship to our little town. It was to see Captain Brown, whom it appears he had known in the wars, and who had somehow saved his lordship's life off the Cape of Good Hope. Knowing Mrs. Jamieson's lack of innocent curiosity you will not be surprised to learn that she could not tell me how the thing occurred. I was curious to know how Captain Brown, with his small house, could put up so distinguished a guest; and I discovered that his lordship slept at the Angel but had his meals with the Browns, during the two days he stayed at Cranford. From the butcher's wife I learn that Miss Jessie bought a leg of lamb, but besides this I can hear of no preparation whatever for so distinguished a visitor. Perhaps the entertainment was mainly intellectual, and we who know Captain Brown's sad want of relish for good English may be glad he has had the opportunity of improving his taste by talking with a cultured nobleman. But who is altogether free from some earthly failings?

(*b*) All that I know is that it is a Miss Hawkins of Bath : but I do not understand how you could hear it, Mr. Knightley; for it is not five minutes since I received Mrs. Cole's note, and the very moment she was told it by her husband she wrote to me.

(*c*) 1. Omit either *annual* or *every year*. 2. The reluctant boy goes to school because he must [*reluctant* cannot be cut out. Though a boy must go to school, it does not follow that he goes reluctantly.] 3. *There's* a type of man that cannot allow that anybody possesses principles for which he is prepared to argue. Such is the base condition of that person standing amongst you that he cannot recognise an honest man when he meets him. 4. Omit *previously*. 5. Omit *downward* or *descending*. 6. Omit any two of the three : *free, gratis, for nothing*. 7. I put on my hat and walked into the Strand. 8. The sentence is useless as it stands. Probably what was meant is : She and her brother are twins. 9. He was mounted on a horse. 10. The defaulter was sent to London by train. 11. This sentence is nonsense. There is no connection between the two clauses. Put a period after *song*. Then add : The air was moist, etc. 12. Omit *elder*. 13. Meaningless as it stands : The sentence means : This picture is beyond comparison the best picture in that gallery. 14. For *make the remark that* substitute *say*.

Exercise 20

1. In every occurrence there are some elements which are recognised by only a few. 2. It would be quite unfair to read party newspapers and form our opinions upon them. 3. Judged from this point of view the picture may present an aspect entirely different from that it presents

to a person without the same knowledge. 4.
We have no universal law to include everything
under its sway [*under its sway* might be with
advantage omitted]. 5. Here *though* suggests
that well-worn grooves are not usually smooth,
which is untrue : *smooth because well-worn* would
be nearer the truth. *Smooth through use* ex-
presses what is meant. 6. The arguments of
each may . . . 7. Omit *without reason* :
mechanism never has reason. 8. *These* data :
data is plural. 9. Omit *and exhaustive,* for
complete includes *exhaustive* 10. Omit *and which
is wrong.* 11. For *them* read *him.* 12. Omit
too much, as these words would imply that we
ought to be somewhat, though not excessively,
prejudiced. 13. *On* or *about* our views. 14.
In thinking or discussion of any sort . . . [The
change is necessary to keep the two important
words together. As the sentence stands *sort*
has too much prominence.] 15. Although two
apparently opposing opinions may be formed
closer examination may show that both are
absolutely correct. 16. The newspaper man puts
in a great many unnecessary details in order to
add to the number of lines, since he is paid at
the rate of a penny per line. [As the sentence
stands it means that the more unnecessary details
he can introduce the greater the number of
pennies paid for each line.] 17. . . . *are* the
same. 18. This sentence is hopeless as it stands.
Observe particularly the vicious repetition of *use.*
Probably the meaning intended may be thus
expressed. The main advantage of political
clubs and literary societies is the practice they
afford in debate. 19. There is no more difficult
thing than to see both sides of a question, or . . .

than to look at a subject from our opponent's standpoint. 20. Seldom do we get any one who thinks exactly like his neighbour, and never do we get many persons who think absolutely alike on a subject. [As the sentence stands it implies that many persons *may* sometimes think absolutely alike, but two persons never.]

Exercise 21

1. Broken construction: omit *at*, or substitute *he* for *there*. 2. Loose participle: After thinking for a long time she hit upon a bright idea. 3. Wrong future: shall I. 4. Wrong sequence of tenses: wished to submit. 5. Since *every* is distributive *health* should be singular: every one may have abilities and live under circumstances, but he can have only one health. 6. Clumsy agreement of verb and noun: It was no joke to feed five score. 7. False reference of other: a fish is not a " beast of the forest ", so omit *other*. 8. Double negative: omit *not*. 9. Loose participle: . . . all turned their thoughts towards supper. 10. Misapplication of word; only creatures having will can be unanimous: There was none that did not admire this poem. 11. Misapplication of word: Through debt he died in poverty. 12. Wrong use of the possessive, and mixed metaphor: We admit the generosity of the gift, but the Town Council in accepting it will, we believe, be found to have made a bad bargain. 13. Lack of proper limitation of statement: Paris is larger than any other city in France. 14. False

agreement : . . . those who cannot describe what they do not see. 15. Wrong order : Three times daily before meals put one of the pills in a little water and swallow it. [Even in this form the *it* is a little ambiguous. The whole sentence should be re-cast.] 16. Tautology : Omit " everything till to-morrow ", or substitute " putting off " for " procrastinating ". 17. Bad arrangement : The sparring with words between Benedick and Beatrice, who says " nobody marks you ", and yet she herself does, makes us wonder how all that will end. [Even when Beatrice and Benedick are brought together the sentence is ill balanced : perhaps " who . . . does " might be marked off by dashes.] 18. Wrong limitation : Little Hop-o'-my-thumb was cleverer than any of his brothers. 19. Misapplication of phrase : We cannot " come between " a marriage . . . she had prevented. 20. Contradiction between the two parts of the sentence : If we let her have her wish there is no need to aid her towards the consummation of it, though we may aid towards the consummation of further wishes.

Exercise 22

(*a*) 1. If this juggler does well I'll get him as high-class an audience as can be attracted here. For my part I always like to praise a poor fellow who does his best, however feeble that best may be ; for there always remains the satisfaction of having done a good turn. To make a poor juggler happy suits my humour more than to see the best juggling in the world. But crowds are ill to please and cruel as the Holy . . . Shall we all go now in company?

2. (A free rendering.) Let but this juggler do well, and I'll get him a first-rate audience. It suits my humour to reward a poor fellow's best. If one has little pleasure in the juggling, one has always the satisfaction of having done a good turn. But crowds are cruel and hard to please. Let us all go in company.

(b) 1. It is worth while repeating the story that old Sir Roger Chamloe, who was at one time Chief Justice, used to tell about himself. When he was Senior Barrister of the Inns of Court he was called upon to deal with some young men who had been guilty of certain misdemeanours. As it was well known that Sir Roger in his youth had been himself a roystering blade, one of the boldest of the culprits pled that they were young fellows, and that wise men before them had sowed their wild oats, and were now none the worse. The knight, however, was equal to the occasion. He admitted that as a youth he had behaved like them, but he pointed out that all his twelve comrades in evil had come to a bad end. Accordingly he urged the delinquents to follow the counsel of his age, rather than the example of his youth, if they had any desire to attain to either his years or his rank, and warned them that their present course was leading straight to poverty, if not indeed to the scaffold.

2. (A free rendering.). Old Sir Roger Chamloe, Chief Justice of England, used to tell how, when he was an official at the Inns of Court, some young fellows were brought before him on a charge of breach of discipline. Their spokes-

man, knowing that Sir Roger had himself had a stormy youth, pled that they were spirited young men and had done no more than many had done before them, without harm to any one. The judge wisely admitted that he himself had erred like them in his youth, but explained that the result in his case was exceptional. He alone of all the band of roystering blades to which he had once belonged had not come to a bad end. He therefore urged the culprits to follow the advice of his mature years rather than the example of his callow youth.

(c) During the fortnight we stayed here our amusements were both numerous and delightful; nothing in fact could be more attractive. Before breakfast we both walked on the pier, my master in a blue marine jacket, and I in a grand new livery. We were both provided with marine binoculars with which we carefully examined the sea and all the petty details connected with it, from the fishwives down to the little waves playing leap frog like children and tumbling over one another in their hurry to get to shore as if anxious to enjoy the peace of dry land.

After breakfast we went down to the beach again, each of us to his own place—for in this foreign town my post involved no work—and examined the marine details as before. This lasted till dinner, and dinner kept us busy till bed-time, and bed-time tided us over till next day, with its breakfast, dinner, and marine details as before. Year in and year out all the people here, including as I am told some ten thousand fortunate English people, lead this pleasant life.

(d) " Well, let it be the presbytery," said I,

for I saw that my wife's patience, none too firm at the best, was giving way. I know exactly how much it will stand, as indeed I ought to by this time. "Well, the court met and was constituted."

"What does that mean?" asked Rob Adair.

"Faith, I don't know. You must ask the clerk. These were his words," said I. "Then there were reports and columns of figures like children's exercises in arithmetic. But nobody attended much and there was a good deal of general conversation till the clerk called out 'Order'. There was silence for half a minute, and then they were all at it again. Indeed the clerk himself talked when he was off his guard."

"Dear me! So that's a presbytery. I thought it was like a week of sacraments!" said my wife.

"Far from that," said I, "for of all fighting creatures pigeons and clergymen are the most quarrelsome."

"Did our minister fight?" asked my wife pointedly.

"No, he was rather a peacemaker in a way," said I cautiously. "Of course a man must sometimes speak his mind."

"Oh, he never does anything wrong, our minister, I understand," replied she drily.

"You surely are not the man to find fault with your own church," said Rob. Sometimes I fear that old Rob is beginning to dote a little.

Exercise 23

Were it true that, given ideas, words will cause no difficulty, it would follow that the most learned man is the most eloquent—a conclusion contrary to experience. Words, as well as matter, demand our attention. Indeed many eminent authors find the effort of expression greater than that of thought. Frequently the lack of a single word necessitates the reconstruction of a whole paragraph, and when all difficulties have been overcome, the result seldom pleases the author.

Exercise 24

Material for essay on Railway Station (arranged according to second method in Lesson XXIV).

1. What does it look like? What general impressions have you? High, murky, smoke-encrusted roof, network of gleaming rails below, trains, great engines vomiting smoke, long grey platforms, porters with trucks, high piles of luggage, waiting taxis, hurrying people, bookstalls, newspaper-boys, chocolate-sellers, perambulating tea-urns, endless crowds, continuous bustle, etc., etc.

2. What is its character and use?

Centre of communications, focus-point of great network of lines, beginning and ending of journeys, home of the engines, importance in commerce and organisation of transport, for the traveller a starting-point of adventure, for the little boy a lasting fascination, etc., etc.

3. What special associations has it for you? (It is only possible here to suggest some associations that may be general.) Starting holidays: luggage, clothes, odd parcels, picnic baskets, excited children, etc.

Returning from holidays : as children, bringing back beloved possessions—spades and buckets, damp seaweed, twisted shells, smooth pebbles, sticky pink rock. The whole family sunburned and somewhat shabby.

Seeing friends off : Embarrassment of finding conversation for the last five minutes, last messages, repeated good-byes, waving of handkerchiefs, etc., etc.

(*Note.*—It is worth while to see how G. K. Chesterton has treated the subject in his essay " On Railway Stations.")

Exercise 25

(*b*) " This must be the place," said Ann as, turning a bend in the lane, they came in sight of a white-washed cottage by the edge of the wood. A straggling hedge screened it in front, and a rusty gate opened on to a gravelled path, leading between empty flower-beds to a faded green front door. It was locked and bolted, but through the uncurtained windows they could peer into a little low-roofed parlour. Plaster, fallen from walls and ceiling, lay thick upon the floor, and a spider had built his web across the empty grate. They tip-toed round to the back. Grass stood high where once the lawn had been, and the lily pond was thick with fallen leaves. The kitchen door stood ajar, for the latch was broken, and brown leaves had drifted in across the floor. A narrow creaking staircase led out of the kitchen, and ended in a dusky passage. There were three small attics and in one of them a long coffin-shaped bath. Ann gazed doubtfully at the cracked, greying paint, the ancient geyser. " H. & C.," said William gloomily. " It's very old-world," said Ann.

(In this description, the details are selected to emphasise the air of dereliction, the rest omitted.)

Exercise 26

In order to see how the subject is treated by a master, turn to Addison's " Adventures of a Shilling " as told by him in the *Tatler*. To begin with, he takes off the edge of the unreality of the composition by making it the outcome of a reverie which " cannot be so properly called a dream as a delirium ". The actual adventure should be read in the original.

Exercise 27

13 INGLEBOROUGH AVENUE,
WIRENCESTER, 16*th July*, 1937.

The Stationmaster,
   L. & N. W. Railway,
      Bletchley.

DEAR SIR,
        To-day I travelled in a third-class compartment in the train leaving Euston at 3 P.M. and reaching Bletchley at 4.58 P.M. Be-

tween these two stations I have lost a silk umbrella. The stick is thin and green; the handle is straight, widening gradually into a silver top, which is not a knob. If it has not turned up at Bletchley, will you please wire to the terminus of the train in question to find whether the umbrella has been found there. I shall be glad to send a postal order for 10s. by way of reward if the umbrella is sent to me at the above address. A note of your expenses in the matter will have my immediate attention.

Yours truly,

GEORGE MAIDENHEAD.

13 INGLEBOROUGH AVENUE,
WIRENCESTER, 16th July, 1937.

DEAR MRS. HICKSON,

Please would you look all through my rooms to make sure that I have not left that new umbrella—with the green stick and the silver top—that came to me by parcel post the other day. If you do find it, make it up into a parcel, and send Susan with it to the Globe Parcel Express in Worcester Road. She knows the place. I enclose an addressed label which you will stick on the parcel. If you do not find the new umbrella do *not* send any of the others.

Yours truly,

GEORGE MAIDENHEAD.

13 INGLEBOROUGH AVENUE,
WIRENCESTER, 16*th July*, 1937.

DEAR JERKYNS,
                    Would you mind taking a look round
in my corner to see if I have left my green-
handled, silver-topped silk umbrella anywhere
about? It is a present from my " expectations "
aunt, who is due at the Rushtons' here on the
18th. I remember that I did not put it in the
stand along with the others, so anxious was I
not to forget it, when I set out for the train in
the afternoon. I have an impression that I had
the wretched thing with me in the train, and that
I put it in the rack. I have written to the railway people, but I write you also as there is no
time to be lost if I am to make a respectable
impression on the 18th. If the thing is lurking
in the neighbourhood of my desk make it worth
Billy's while to send it here by passenger train,
and charge the damages to me.
                                    Yours ever,
                                    G. MAIDENHEAD.

13 INGLEBOROUGH AVENUE,
WIRENCESTER, 16*th July*, 1937.

MY DEAR VI.,
                    I wonder if you remember the gamp
Aunt Matilda gave me on my birthday—thin
green stick, straight top, silver-tipped (just like
yours, only thicker and less silver), silk stuff.
Well, so far as I can make out, it is now lost.
Of course she bought it at Akenside's. There

must be others of the same kind in stock. If you get a wire from me to-morrow with the message *buy*, then go straight to Akenside's, buy as near a match to the lost umbrella as you can get, and get him to send it to me here by passenger train (Midland). If you don't get a wire by noon, that will mean that the lost umbrella has turned up.

The enclosed P.O.O. for 30s. is all I can afford to send. I am sure the wretched thing did not cost more, but at any price I must have a duplicate before I can face the old lady on Thursday.

Now, *don't* buy an umbrella or do anything more in the matter unless you get a wire. If the thing turns up you may keep the 30s. for your honesty.

Yours ever,
GEORGE.

In these letters there is a difference in tone corresponding to the relation between Maidenhead and his correspondent. The station-master and the landlady are not at all interested in Maidenhead's reason for recovering the umbrella; so no mention is made of the aunt. Inexperienced writers often expose themselves to ridicule by putting unnecessary details into letters to strangers. Jerkyns himself should not be told about the aunt unless Maidenhead and he are on very friendly terms. Even here, how-ever, it is well to avoid naming her. In writing to the sister, Maidenhead might have omitted the slang term " gamp "; but in familiar letters we must not be pedantic so long as clearness is not sacrificed. It is a wise rule, all the same, to avoid any expression about the propriety of which you have any doubt. The very fact that you question the fitness of an expression should condemn that expression. Note too the different directions about how the umbrella is to be sent, if found. The stationmaster gets no instructions at all; Jerkyns merely gets the hint to send it by passenger train. The clerk is supposed to know how to despatch a parcel, but the landlady gets minute directions, while the sister is told to get the shopman to send the umbrella.

Exercise 28

See Leigh Hunt's essay on this same subject, which he treats from a very personal standpoint.

Exercise 29

(a) THE RENAISSANCE.

I. New birth of the world beginning about middle of fifteenth century.

> Two previous but minor Renaissances.

>> (1) Time of Charlemagne.
>> (2) Thirteenth century.

II. Causes—

> A. Immediate—Taking of Constantinople and scattering of Greek scholars.

B. Ultimate—

   (1) Invention of printing and consequent spread of inquiry.
   (2) Invention of gumpowder and consequent fall of feudalism.
   (3) Progress of geographical discovery and consequent breadth of view.

III. Results—

   A. Broadening of interests.
   B. Recognition of the solidarity of humanity.

IV. The passing of the new spirit—end of Renaissance.

   A. Mistaking the letter for the spirit.
   B. Reformers became bigots, and scholars became pedants.

(b) THE EXCEPTION PROVES THE RULE.

I. As commonly used this proverb is false. Example: the rule *No quadruped lays eggs* is disproved by the exception *Crocodiles lay eggs*.

II. Distinction between two ways of regarding proverb.

   A. Inductively: Passing from examples to the rule.
      Here the proverb is false.
   B. Deductively: Passing from the rules to examples.
      Here the proverb is true.

222

III. Deduction does not express the exception as such.

> Good boys die young—adjective *good* excepts all other boys.
> Therefore we have the rule proved—bad boys do not die young.

IV. Silliness of the proverb as usually used.
> When used inductively very misleading.
> When used deductively tends to clear expression.

Exercise 30

SHAKESPEARE'S TREATMENT OF THE SUPERNATURAL

" After God, Shakespeare created most." For once, an epigram speaks true. Hugo's phrase conjures up an infinite company—Hamlet sad-coated, Lear " fantastically crowned ", Falstaff and Prince Hal sauntering arm-in-arm, Shylock and Antonio, Beatrice, Benedick, Bottom the Weaver. . . . They are shadows, yet more real than life; their vitality is greater than our own. And what of the other creatures of his creation—ghosts and witches haunting the confines of darkness, Warwickshire fairies, brutish Caliban, delicate Ariel? In the supernatural world, Shakespeare's imagination moves most freely. So long as men and women are the subjects of his art, the dramatist is limited by all the imperfections of humanity; but in fairyland and the dread domain of the weird sisters he can give full scope to his imagination. It has been complained of Shakespeare that he makes his characters of every age and country express themselves in the forms of his own time, and there is of necessity an element of truth in the objection. But in the supernatural world all this is changed. Nature is jealous of the copyright of humanity, but the poet may evade her claims by crossing Styx, just as the publisher evades the poet's by crossing the Atlantic.

Living in the world Shakespeare was emphatically of the world. He had none of your philosopher's contempt for mere earthly things, yet he dearly loved a flight into cloudland. In such flights he carried with him his broad human sympathies, and imparted to the airy nothings just so much of human nature as rendered them intelligible to ordinary men. It is true that there are some men who do not consider themselves " ordinary ", to whom all that is not tangible or demonstrable is folly. For such matter-of-fact philosophers is the apologetic tone of *A Midsummer Night's Dream* intended. But Shakespeare has his revenge, for the dullards who could see nothing but childishness in the fairy gambols were led to laugh at their own reflection in " sweet bully Bottom " and his friends.

In giving a kind of reality to the supernatural agents, Shakespeare has, as elsewhere, seized upon the universal side of his subject. " In literature as in love," says Heine, " the secret of success is to dare." Who would now dare to introduce a real live fairy into poem or novel? Yet now, as in Shakespeare's time, men have a hungering after the supernatural. Every one with imagination enough " to raise the ghost of a fishwife " would like to believe in fairyland,

and secretly resents the cold insensibility with which Reason explains away Titania and all her train. On this point modern writers have made a compromise, which, as is natural, satisfies neither reason nor fancy. Who does not remember the rude shock which his credulity—the charm of childhood—received on first reading at the end of a thrilling tale of enchantment the depressing sentence—" And I awoke ". Heine himself, daring as he is in other fields, often thus falls asleep over his lyrics. Shakespeare, however, introduces us to no mere shades. Titania and Oberon are as real to us as Joan of Arc and Hotspur. In *A Midsummer Night's Dream* the fairies are but human beings whose smaller growth is compensated by increased powers. They must use means to attain their ends, and though the means be powerful they sometimes bungle their application. Oberon sets himself up as a kind of Providence to " human mortals ", and is sadly perplexed at the peculiar results of his good intentions. Puck confesses that " fate o'er-rules ", and thus establishes a bond of sympathy between the spirits and those mortals at whose folly he laughs. The fairies do not derive their interest merely from their influence on the other characters, they are in themselves attractive. Shakespeare lets us into the secret of all the intrigues of fairyland, but the disclosure of the hidden springs which move the natural and supernatural world of Athens, far from destroying the interest, lends a new charm to the whole.

A Midsummer Night's Dream marks the highest point to which the mere fairy of literature ever attained. Before this play, the fairy had too close a connection with the hobgoblin; after it the progress of higher education not only predisposed men to disbelieve in fairies, but actually corrupted the fairies themselves. When we find them singing Latin songs,[1] we are in some sort prepared for the shock of recognising Oberon's legitimate descendants in the monstrosities in " ism " and " ation " which tantalise the readers of " instructive books for the young ".

By as much as the ethereal Puck transcends the gross Robin Goodfellow of popular superstition with his coarse Ho! ho! ho! by so much does Ariel transcend Puck. Puck may be said to be, in the language of popular novelists, founded upon fact, Ariel is a pure creation of the fancy. In however short a time Puck can girdle the earth, he is but an agent to carry out the directions of his master, and blunders even in that. Ariel has merely to be told what Prospero wishes, and it is accomplished with " no mistakings ". Yet Ariel is but Puck caught, tamed and educated. The spirit now " tricksy " in his master's interest was formerly mischievous enough in his own, and his true nature is shown in the use he makes of his liberty. He lapses into the fairy life from which Prospero's art had for a while withdrawn him. *The Tempest* is indeed the converse of *A Midsummer Night's Dream.* Man and fairy change places. Prospero dethrones Oberon and himself assumes the part of Providence. This combination of natural and supernatural forces is powerful but not all powerful. Charles Lamb is disappointed that Prospero went quietly into the boat without at least raising a storm or two; and certainly it

[1] Randolph's *Amyntas* (1640 A.D.).

seems strange that nearly twenty years should be allowed to elapse before the " so potent art " was put in operation against the usurper. But it must be remember that had Prospero been omnipotent there would have been no tale to tell.

Perhaps there is no other play of Shakespeare's in which the ideal meaning is so conspicuous as in *The Tempest*. Ariel represents the imagination of man in its widest sense—scientific as well as poetic. We have here man triumphing over nature, as in *A Midsummer Night's Dream* we have man subject to nature. It may be said that the liberation of Ariel spoils all these fine theories, and in a sense this is true. But the breakdown in the hidden meaning arises from the harmony of the story, and is really one of the beauties of the play, illustrating as it does one of the finest characteristics of Shakespeare. He is an artist first, a moralist or a philosopher only in the second place. The " dainty Ariel " would have been utterly out of place in the civic life of Milan, hence he was liberated, and the moral was left to take care of itself. In fact Shakespeare's hidden meanings were intended only for men with intelligence enough to take them in as a whole. To such minds hints are sufficient, the details can be easily filled in. Some characters in the plays indeed seem to have many meanings which may be read in them, to say nothing of those which may be read into them. Caliban represents the untutored savage drinking the " water with berries in it ", brutalised humanity, and evil forces as opposed to the good in Ariel. All these points are hinted at in the play, but none of them is brought into such prominence that the unity of the story is at all marred.

The simple man reads it as a story, and is satisfied.

Even this subordinate degree of undermeaning detracts from the artistic value of the work. The highest poetry is that which combines reality and ideality : the poem must be perfectly ideal and yet accepted as true. This is recognised even in the nursery, where the question, " Is it true? " must be answered in the affirmative before the promised story has much chance of success. A boy by a strong effort of the imagination can realise to himself Swift's Lilliputians and Yahoos. Explain the satire, and the boy's mind becomes divided between real Yahoos and shadowy abstractions, and finally falls back upon his faithful Crusoe, of whose existence he has no doubt. In the same way, though in a less degree, we are disturbed in our belief in the reality of Prospero and his powers.

All this is changed when we consider Shakespeare's ghosts. They have no secret meaning, they come for a definite purpose, accomplish it, and are gone. Again they appeal to a more universal instinct than do the fairies. It is a part of man's nature to seek to pry into futurity, to seek to know something of that great unknown land to which we are all journeying. Besides, Shakepeare's ghosts no more resemble those of our churchyards than Titania the fairy of common superstition. The ghost in *Hamlet* is no white-sheeted spectre, but a majestic warrior wearing a well-known suit of armour. Banquo's ghost is but Banquo invisible to all save Macbeth. It is true that in the interest of reality the former is subject to the insulting power of chanticleer, and is condemned " to walk the night ", though why he should object to a cool walk on a breezy night after a day spent in "sulphurous and tormenting flames" is not set forth. Such ghosts, and those that appear in *Richard III.* and *Julius Cæsar*, are quite conceivable. They represent persons who once lived upon this earth, and moreover their common purpose is distinctly human—revenge. They all come of their own accord, at any rate, no human influence calls them up. Though they come, however, with a common purpose, they do not seek it by a common method. Hamlet's father hands over the business to his son. Julius Cæsar merely intimates disaster, but he appears personally to his enemy; the ghosts in *Richard III.* simply give utterance to their good and bad wishes; Banquo alone says nothing, yet he has most effect. Only in *Hamlet* and *Macbeth* is the ghost of paramount importance, in the other two cases it is a mere incident.

Compared with the fairies the ghosts command readier belief, but they fail on their ideal side. Like photographs they are too true to life—to real life, not to ghost life—but this is compensated for by the use made of them. Unlike the fairies they are in themselves unattractive, and we are interested in them only in so far as they affect the characters in the play. They are but means; the fairies are both means and ends. The ghosts are placed before us with no character save that which they carried with them from this life, with no apparent relation to spirit-land, or at least none that they are allowed to explain; in short they merely appear in order to finish off those tag ends of life which their hurried departure prevented them from attending to. They act on the same principles as those on which we should expect them to act were Shakespeare, like Scott in a notable case, to call back any of them from the dead. Hamlet could have been made to discover for himself the treachery of the new King, yet there is no waste of spiritual energy in the play. Whatever else the author wished to express he certainly intended to draw a picture of the most pronounced irresolution, and for this the ghost was a most useful instrument. Hamlet disbelieved in the ghost till he saw it : even after seeing it he doubted the truth of its utterances, and this doubt is at the root of the movement of half the play. Banquo's ghost has no such outstanding part to perform, it merely takes its place in a whole world of horrors.

The witches occupy an intermediate place between the fairies and the ghosts : they are in themselves more interesting than the latter and less interesting than the former. In *Macbeth* the witches have some system of organisation the exact nature of which is artistically suppressed. Philosophy is mingled with the loathsome gibberish of their rites, and their aims are higher than to crook an arm or waste a liver. They hunt not bodies, but souls. It has been ingeniously suggested that the witches are three in number because they represent past, present and future time—Glamis, Cawdor, King; and there is nothing against the hypothesis. Three is a convenient number, a mystic number, an odd number, and " Witchcraft loveth numbers odd ". In a tragic work like *Macbeth* it is important to introduce the supernatural in its most plausible form, and nowhere has Shakepeare been more successful than here. The English nation were prepared to believe in fairies and ghosts, but they felt bound to believe in witches. To deny their existence was blasphemy: were they not mentioned in Scripture? In 1584 Reginald Scot in his *Discovery of Witchcraft* maintains that people would have believed as strongly in fairies as in witches were it not that "it hath not pleased the translators of the Bible to call spirits by the name of Robin Goodfellow".

With these awful powers, then, Shakespeare opens *Macbeth*. Whence they come and wherefore is left untold. All that we know is that they are seeking to obtain the soul of the honourable and courageous general, Macbeth. The weird sisters may be regarded at the beginning of the play as the fates, at the end as the furies. Yet with all their power they are not absolute : "amen" is not the only word with which man may reply to their machinations. Nor can they be even said to fight unfairly against humanity : they tell no lies. If Macbeth fall he must blame his interpretation, not their statements. Like Mephistopheles in Marlowe's *Faust* they seem to be compelled, however much against their will, to speak the truth, even at the risk of breaking the fifth commandment. The subordinate apparitions are in perfect keeping with traditional witchcraft, and with the *motif* of the play. It would be rash to assert dogmatically what Shakespeare meant to express in *Macbeth* ; yet to a mind like his, delighting to toy with intellectual edge-tools, nothing could be more attractive than the ever-present question of fate and freewill. Instead of trying to solve the insoluble problem by a quarrel with some neighbour, he quietly writes a drama of thrilling interest for every one, in which is contained an example of the harmonious action of fate and freewill. Macbeth is quite evidently doomed from the first, yet at no point can we stop and say that here he was forced to act thus and thus. This may seem rather a frivolous view of a very solemn question, but it certainly is in keeping with Shakespeare's character. He knew too well the difficulties of a question to answer it absolutely one way or another.

Be this as it may, it is certain that the play does not suffer for the sake of the moral. But besides this artistic indifference to " leading ideas ", which we have marked throughout, there is another peculiarity in Shakespeare's treatment of the supernatural—it is always used in an organic relation to the development of the plot.

A very effective use is sometimes made of the supernatural in supplying a suitable setting for certain incidents. A notable case is found in *Julius Cæsar*, where Casca's description of the weird sights he has seen prepares a fitting atmosphere for the events that are to follow. So with the comet brandishing its crystal tresses in the sky " importing change of times and states ". Full well Shakespeare knew the power of the materials he used :—

" Look how the poor world's people are amaz'd
At apparitions, signs and prodigies ".

Still more important is the use Shakespeare makes of the supernatural in developing character. In few ways can we get more directly at a man's character than by a study of his superstitions. The fiends that appear to Joan of Arc in the first part of *Henry VI.* are really symbols to express the popular estimate of her character, and of the English gallantry which could overcome both man and devil. Shakespeare does not make her a witch in revenge for her victories over the English, but because she was burned as a witch, and that—in the popular opinion of his time—justly. The spirit raised by Bolingbroke in the second part of *Henry VI.* is a counterpart of the " juggling fiends " of *Macbeth*. Throughout this play there runs a thread of poetic cursing that reminds one of Gray's " Bard ". The curse and its effect are skilfully varied as speaker and hearer change. The wild Celtic egotism of Owen Glendower is developed in a special kind of superstition which glorifies himself and ruins his fellow rebels. The same fitness in the supernatural relations of men and shades is maintained through all the plays. The King, cut off in his sins, is " doomed" to walk. Banquo's ghost has a kind of ghastly enjoyment in shaking his gory locks at his murderer, but the gracious Duncan is too good to be compelled to return from the spirit world, and too gentle to return of his own accord to increase Macbeth's misery.

INDEX

234

c